P9-CAG-669

WITHDRAWN

THE SPACE BETWEEN

THE
SPACE
BETWEEN

LITERATURE AND POLITICS

JAY CANTOR

THE JOHNS HOPKINS UNIVERSITY PRESS

BALTIMORE AND LONDON

"The Red Wheelbarrow" is from *Collected Earlier Poems,* by William
Carlos Williams, copyright 1938 by New Directions Publishing Corp.
It is reprinted here by permission of New Directions.

This book was brought to publication with the generous
assistance of the Andrew W. Mellon Foundation.

Copyright © 1981 by Jay Cantor
All rights reserved
Printed in the United States of America

The Johns Hopkins University Press, Baltimore, Maryland 21218
The Johns Hopkins Press Ltd., London

Library of Congress Cataloging in Publication Data

Cantor, Jay.
  The space between.

  Bibliography: p. 159
  1. Politics and literature. I. Title.
PN51.C333   809'.93358   81-47600
ISBN 0-8018-2672-1   AACR2

PN
51
.C333

FOR MY PARENTS

3/4/83   ᴸB

CONTENTS

FOREWORD

No other book I know puts things together quite in the way of Jay Cantor's *The Space Between: Literature and Politics.* Its essays, working against and for one another, are displaced from the usual haunts and habits of literary or political prose. I think I can most usefully provide an introduction to them by indicating how they have encouraged me to place myself with respect to them, in terms of them.

My sixties began in the early summer of 1964 in Mississippi and ended in the late summer of 1974 with the television coverage of Richard Nixon's farewell to his White House staff. Whether one considers those years to have been hopeful or hateful ones, there can be few periods in any nation's experience in which more of its people have questioned or revised its identity for themselves. Call such periods crises of imagination. I know of no such crisis that remains so poorly grasped. That poorness must itself be part of what constitutes this crisis.

One may describe Jay Cantor's *The Space Between: Literature and Politics* as an effort to imagine that time, and therewith an effort to grasp ours as a time for imagining. It is also about what must constitute such imagination, and about why it must consider that constitution, what kind of writing it is that shoulders it. It is about being born around 1950 (hence, having to grow through adolescence within the dates I called the sixties) and about conceiving and accepting the ambition, in those years, to be a writer. I understand this nesting of subjects in the way I would understand Wordsworth's *Prelude* to be simultaneously about being born in 1770 (hence, being nineteen in 1789) and about accepting the

ambition to be a writer in those years of English writing. Each
of these writers is claiming that ambitious writing in his time must
shoulder the imagination and the acknowledgment of his time,
where this is considered to mean not just knowing a thing or two
about the time and about writing, but also seeing the public and his
private history as one and the same nesting of subjects. Hegel, also
born in 1770, expressed this knowledge another way, call it dialectically; Thoreau, sensing other revolutions, expressed it scripturally.
All tend toward the autobiographical.

Accomplishing the conjunction of private and public history—call this composing the autobiography of your times—demands
a healthy respect for your capacity to write. Jay Cantor is also the
writer of a long novel in progress, two excerpts of which have been
published.* The rim of the novel's subject is the life and works of
Che Guevara, identified in *The Space Between: Literature and
Politics* as the subject of one of its periodic pin-up posters, from
whose journal the second excerpt of Jay Cantor's novel intermittently
quotes. In one of these quotes Guevara appears, depicting himself
in a conversation about how commitment to guerrillas may be
expressed, and he says to his journal parenthetically: "The basis of
a first commitment is a very good imagination so you can at least
dream the dangers you are entertaining. I need a batallion of dream-
ers?" Then a few dozen pages later in the novel, a key associate of
Guevara's, the writer Regis Debray, is saying to a fellow revolutionary
that words have their time in a revolutionary process, and the fellow
replies: "I came to understand what those feelings I had meant in
my world. There's room for words. There have to be words, too. But
that isn't the way it started for me. When I listen to you, I don't
know. Can it start out as thinking?" That is a beautiful use of Hem-
ingway "it," meaning here the revolution, but no less meaning one's
writing, and no less the seriousness, the thoughtfulness, of one's
life, or the moment at which, as Conrad (I think) puts it, the pos-
sibility of a moral existence begins or ends.

It seems to me that Jay Cantor's writing is characterizing
itself as the commitment "to dream the dangers we are entertaining."

Tri Quarterly 45 (Spring 1979): 199–237; and *Canto* 1, no. 4 (Winter 1977):
1–18.

In writing, as in everyday life, these are not future dangers but present ones, ones inevitable if you are to demand thoughtfulness of your life. Thoreau says in *Walden*, "You may sit as many risks as you run"—you needn't look for moral adventure, it will find you if you are serious. Whether there will be what the world calls a revolution in a particular place is a function of whether there is a revolutionary situation in that place. This is never certain. What is certain is that the possession of oneself, the self's birth of freedom, now presents itself, as nations have presented themselves for two centuries, in terms of revolution, a splitting and struggle for one's own ground. I have expressed something like this thought as a matter of modern philosophy's availability to us only through conversion. But whether as the trope of political revolution or as the trope of religious conversion, the idea, variously expressed in the radical vision of every major philosopher since Bacon and Descartes, is that one finds one's own world only by turning, a turning away from the world (which therefore presents itself as appearance or fashion) that constitutes one's own turning toward a world (which accordingly presents itself, if in the future, as reality or permanence).

I suppose the development of the wish for change into a visionary craving for revolution or conversion is the work of two contrary pieces of knowledge, keeping one another alive: first, the knowledge of oneself, however affable, as enraged and desperate at the state of the world, a rage away from the violent and insupportable narcissism of those in power over us, a despair at one's powerlessness to matter; and second, the knowledge that change must be possible but that, since others will not change, one must make something happen, one must *make* a start, in thoughts, in words, in deeds, so one must become a poet to survive.

Jay Cantor's vision leads through territories unpleasant and frightening to contemplate: Che Guevara, the Patricia Hearst story, the aesthetics of Harold Rosenberg and of Herbert Marcuse, the bits of truth in a hundred more or less, most and least, articulate places. But had one expected to find a better world without knowing the bad of this one, without knowing the bad in the good of it and the good in the bad of it? Then I recommend attention to what I understand as a climax of the vision of *The Space Between: Literature and Politics,* in a brilliant and convincing piece of, let me say, literary criticism. It finds, at the close of a chapter of "notes" on Beckett, that only after despair and equally only after hope can one discover what it is on which our existence—using what may in our boredom have seemed the boring word in William Carlos Williams's poem about the wheel barrow in the rain—depends.

And I recommend attention to the continuity of *The Space Between: Literature and Politics* with such a work as E. M. Forster's *Howards End,* which seems so congenial or genial by comparison. I wonder why people find Forster's epigraph to his masterpiece— "Only connect . . . ."—a profound sentiment. It is taken from the opening paragraphs of chapter 22: "Only connect! That was the whole of her sermon. Only connect the prose and the passion, and both will be exhaulted, and human love will be seen at its height. Live in fragments no longer. Only connect, and the beast and the monk, robbed of the isolation that is life to either, will die." That is not a prediction but a prophecy, a vision. Does it seem genial because it is imagined that the business of connecting is pretty, that it may not exact ugliness and violence in its achieving? The imagined sermon is directed to one who

> always had the sneaking belief that bodily passion is bad, a belief that is desirable only when held passionately. Religion had confirmed him. The words that were read aloud on Sunday to him and to other respectable men were the words that had once kindled the souls of St. Catherine and St. Francis into a white-hot hatred of the carnal. He could not be as the saints and love the infinite with a seraphic ardour, but he could be a little ashamed of loving a wife.

The sixties is the name of a time in which for certain people, for quite a large number of people at certain times, white-hot hatred and seraphic ardor seemed again practical emotions. If, as I do, you understand the religious sects of the seventies as fragmentary successors of the political sects of the sixties, and hence understand that there was from the beginning a religious ground in the student movement—religious yearning, a religious purity, religious corruption and intolerance (there were riots of holiness on both sides, on all sides)—then you may think you can spot the continuity of seraphic ardor. But you must then ask what happened to the white-hot hatred. Could Richard Nixon really have absorbed it all and carried it away into the California desert?

Suppose you can no longer believe in the practicality of these hatreds and ardors *and* you cannot believe in the practices and words that deny so much as their fragmentary revelations (and these words are spoken not only on Sunday but on every day and every night). Suppose you believe at most in the merely human carry of your words, and you wish to lift them merely to lift others, not to seek some transcendent orbit. Then you will have, as befits philosophical prose, to distinguish, to split, as well as to connect. And you will try, as I understand Jay Cantor to do, to connect, to try to achieve a vision in which to connect the prose and the passion, of course (though now that connection sounds rather like an invitation to write a novel—and perhaps, understood usefully, one might after all get a grasp of one's life by taking it as a tale in which you are the narrative voice), and in which to connect the beast and the monk in yourself, of course (though now you will suggest that to accomplish this you must connect the victim and the terrorist in yourself, and the boredom and the poetry, and the prisoner and the judge, and the patriot and the traitor, and the immigrant and the American, and the ardor and the hatred and the craving to write).

At Harvard in the spring of 1969 some hundreds of students were forcibly removed from an administration building by greater hundreds of police. It was several months earlier that I had become aware of Jay Cantor. He had written a feature for the Harvard *Crimson* in response to a student sit-it at a faculty meeting, arguing in effect that in a bad time people on opposite sides of a public issue are equally apt to behave badly, and that each side of the current issue still had an opportunity to turn the other cheek. His statement remains in my mind as the best public statement made in those times, but his eloquent appeal to the best on all sides went unanswered. By the following spring the situation had deteriorated. I was giving a course that spring on texts from Luther and Machiavelli and Shakespeare through Locke and Marx and Mill and through Hume and Kant to Nietzsche and Beckett. Hundreds of students were enrolled in the course, some of whom would have been in the administration building the morning it was emptied, more of whom would have attended the meeting the night before the building was filled, at which a majority had voted—in the largest and most thoroughly democratic meeting of its kind I ever witnessed—not to mount an occupation. Accordingly, some half of the students inside the building the next morning were there to argue the other half into leaving. Did those who used the police know that? If they knew, would they have acted as they did regardless? Why? Because students have no business holding a meeting—however democratically conducted, even seraphically—to discuss a proposal to act illegally? Then why did they hold it, hardly a scene producible by everyday lawbreakers? Did my beautiful list of readings for my course contain terms in which to think this over? And if it did, were they terms that were common to those inside and those outside that building, so they might figure in an argument between them? If not, what does it mean to call a place a university?

The last of the major disruptions of that spring was a week-long strike of classes called by an organization of Teaching Fellows. The following week, as I was collecting myself to go to the classroom and resume the course, there was talk that some Teaching Fellows and some students in the course wanted to continue the strike. As had become second nature to us within the span of a few weeks, we gathered at once for a meeting. I said that for my part I was not prepared to discuss the issue of continuing the strike, that I was going to the classroom and that the other teachers present would have to decide without me what they had to do. One of the most fervent supporters of the idea of the strike then said that this course was certainly special, that it should not be struck any longer, because its reading had suddenly become amazingly relevant. The teacher's heart in me sank. I said something to the effect that I had been assigning roughly the same texts since the beginning of my involvement with the course, half a dozen years earlier, that these texts had always been relevant to our lives, as relevant as thinking about our lives, and that our present events did not serve to show that the world and these texts may illuminate one another but rather that they may eclipse one another.

Now I add that my heart had sunk under the sense of hopelessness of ever really connecting the prose and the passion, the idea of our history with our history as we are making it, of ever having a voice in our history. So our ideas and our histories, separated, fragmented, each eclipse us. We remain essentially uneducated. Those who may share this sense or vision require words for it. I am grateful for the words Jay Cantor has found. I expect him to be recognized as one of the significant voices of his generation. The appearance of his sequence of essays does for me what Emerson asked of the American scholar: it raises and cheers me.

STANLEY CAVELL

ACKNOWLEDGMENTS

These essays are part of the conversations—the shared fears and occasional wonders—of my last decade. They are my part in those talks, and so they have been very much shaped by the curve of other voices, the questions asked, the startling responses offered. Sometimes, though not often enough, some of the other voices of those years appear here, as one might repeat the particularly interesting words a friend says, in order to share in the pleasure of the discovery. It was, as it says in my introduction, Norman Brown's words that opened new fields for my thinking in this period, and new ways of exploring those fields. (The manner and the matter of course came together.) Often, as I made my way into what I thought were unknown continents, I met Norman Brown on his way back. But he was always happy to share in the joys of his adventures, while shouldering most of the costs himself. C. L. Barber's warm encouraging voice is everywhere present here. I wish only that my work might have shown more of his profound care for the continuities of life. Joe's students, readers, and friends know the remarkable depth of his affection and his intelligence, an undivided always active sensibility. Herbert Marcuse gave me, as he has many others, vivid possibilities for argument, for the dialectical battle that he always thought might yield truth (no matter how undistinguished his opponent). Gregory Bateson's work, and his presence, allowed me to glimpse the coherence of the larger "pattern which connects," the natural history that contains us. My friends Carter Wilson and Pam Matz, my companions during many of these years, know how much of our late night conversations, our mixed excited voices and freeing laughter has found its way into these essays. And Jerry Neu provided many difficult points for reconsideration. During the completion of the work, a time of doubts and rewriting, Stanley Cavell's voice, his ability to imagine a setting for remarks of one's own that have grown obscure to oneself, and so clarify them, provided invaluable help. Frank Bidart's extraordinary attention to the manuscript, to the argument and its embodiment, has enriched this book. My thanks to all of them for seeing around things with me, for seeing through some of them, and for seeing me through.

INTRODUCTION:
ECCENTRIC
PROPOSITIONS

HISTORY AND READING

In the late 1960s, during the war in Vietnam, I—like so many people—wanted a political literature, and wanted to read literature politically.

A political literature would be, I thought, a literature that was an instrument of the struggle. This literature could, of course, depending on one's views of the struggle, take different forms: Critical Realism, Socialist Realism, Brecht's Epic Theater—all were formulations of what kind of art would best serve the revolution. And—as the example of Brecht's work showed—political literature could, at least from some perspectives, be an adventurous business, technically innovative. Art, like Brecht's (or even that of an "uncommitted" writer like Joyce in *Ulysses*), that was self-reflexive, concerned with how we order reality, make our world, deceive ourselves or are deceived, could serve a useful demythifying function, one that was—according to this sense of things—potentially revolutionary. Such art revealed to us the kinds of manipulation we were constantly subjected to. It criticized our perceptual habits. It severed us from the myths we were deluded by. It cleared the vision, and so cleared the ground for action.

The right way to read a work, to make it politically valuable (and soon no other kind of value was recognized), was to find its political content. This finding might require an economic, philosophical, or scientific analysis of some sophistication. Yet the work, under this analysis, tended to reveal to us such truths as that the world is divided into classes. That is: the knowledge gained from the work usually preceded the reading, was embedded in the political theory we assumed for ourselves—though perhaps in an abstract

3

form for which the art work might provide a concrete, experiential, subjective example. Proceeding this way one found everywhere, in every work, a confirmation of what one already knew. "The petit-bourgeois," Roland Barthes wrote, " is a man unable to imagine the Other. If he comes face to face with him he blinds himself, ignores and denies him, or else transforms him into himself. In the petit-bourgeois universe all experiences of confrontation are reverberating, any experience of otherness is reduced to sameness."

Perhaps the difficulty for art could be put like this: even giving a greater role to the cultural revolution—a leading one—still the goal is already known; everything falls into place in relation to the goal. (The projection of a known goal, a hope toward which history is marching, is what is crucial for Georg Lukács in defining the difference between the well-formed world of the Critical Realist and the world of decadent writing.) Although Marxist theory was essentially complete, one wanted to improve it a little, to add more territories to it; one wanted to add the subjective, the psychological, the existential, the symbolic. Behind this desire for theoretical aggrandizement was, at best, the intention to improve the theory (but not to reformulate it; practice—changing the world—was never truly open towards activity, never became praxis; theory was always dominant). One wanted to make Marxist theory more complete, more attractive, to add new values, though the sense was that such values—more humane ones—could be added as products to a shopping cart, without changing the theory or the theoretician; at worst the intention was to gain skills from art, knowledge of symbols, techniques of presentation, of manipulation of the symbolic (as if symbols could be manipulated from without, not changing the manipulator).

I will call this manner of reading allegorical—following a simple or complicated system of transformations known before confronting the text—to find out that what one already knew, had projected by one's manner of enquiry, by the shape of one's questioning, was in the text. The method does not seem a very satisfactory way to proceed either for art or politics. Read in this way no work can change one's ideas; art provides neither seeds nor moisture.

Nor, given Marxist political theory, should we expect it to. Art is part of the superstructure, and although relations between the superstructure and the base are very complicated, dialectically interactive; still it is the base, the infrastructure, that is in the last instance determinant of one's ideas, one's consciousness—not art. And the base is known, comes to consciousness, only in Marxist science. As Herbert Marcuse has written, "The basic structure and dynamic of society can never find sensuous aesthetic expression; they are in Marxian theory the essence behind the appearance, which can only be attained through scientific analysis and formulated only in terms of that analysis."

FIGHTING SELF; OR, DESPAIR

That art should provide seeds of new ideas, new ways of feeling, new consciousness, is not, of course, a traditional Marxist demand on the art work. (In fact, as it is the base which produces consciousness, that is an impossible demand.) "The philosophers," Marx wrote in the last of his *Thesis on Feuerbach,* "have *interpreted* the world in various ways; the point is to *change* it." The Left had taken this to heart. One went to the work of art (or to the masses), whether to the creation of a work or its reading, with the problem already known and well defined, and with the solution to the problem already known, the solution provided by Marxist science. The solution need not be stated; again, it is projected within the method used, the form of the question asked. This reading for the already known remains fundamentally unchanged in the work of such contemporary Marxists as Pierre Macherey (*A Theory of Literary Production*) or Terry Eagleton (*Criticism and Ideology*). Though there is here an emphasis on the literary activity, the activity always produces an ideological product, or effect, already known. The silences, or contradictions of the text speak; from them we learn that George Eliot was petit-bourgeois, and that the petite-bourgeoisie could not resolve certain contradictions, say certain necessary words, fill certain silences. But this was known, of course, before we read George Eliot.

But many came to feel that one could not move toward the world with already known solutions. Rather, oneself was part of the world that required changing. What Nietzsche had written of Christian ethics applied also to Marxist ethics; the dissolution of that ethic would be caused by its being followed through to its conclusion, by its being held to rigorously. Unable to tolerate any untruth, the Christian world, Nietzsche said, following its own ethic of scrupulous honesty, would eventually turn upon itself, dissatisfied with its own sham. So, too, the Marxist must, and often did, turn upon himself. One's politics, if held to, would have one see oneself as unworthy, bourgeois, as part of the world that needed changing.

There would be then a necessary shift in one's thinking a shift brought about perhaps by the extremity of one's guilty condition. But eventually this sense of guilt (and the sense also— a sense for which art must be partly responsible—that other states of consciousness were possible) must find its goal in the sacrifice of oneself, of one's ego, in, as Brecht says in *The Baden Learning Play,* "giving oneself up."

The Learned Chorus:	If you have improved the world, Then improve the world you have improved. Give it up!
The Leader of the Learned Chorus:	Forward march!
The Learned Chorus:	If improving the world, you have perfected truth, Then perfect the truth you have perfected. Give it up!

. . . .

If perfecting the truth, you have changed
   mankind,
Then change the mankind you have changed.
Give it up!

. . . .

Changing the world, change yourselves!
Give yourselves up!

If there was a world to be changed, a new world to be made (a new world, as W. C. Williams wrote, is a new mind), then we were not, as we found ourselves, capable of making it; the self that should be expressed in that building—that would we thought direct it, for we still

thought of it as a matter of "self-expression"—was not yet a satisfactory self. In fact, thinking this through to its conclusion, we
were not even capable of seeing the work that needed to be done,
for we were (as one Red Guard wrote during the Chinese Cultural
Revolution) "blinded by the bourgeois self."

> The fight against the bourgeois ideas in our own heads, the fight against
> self is much the same. The "self" within us is like this omnipresent
> glue which persistently tries to twist each of our thoughts into some-
> thing useful to it. Only by continuous struggle against this glue and
> constant vigilance as to its tricks can we keep ourselves moving forward
> on the road to revolution. . . .
>
> But there is more to this question of self. It . . . is also like blinders
> on our own eyes. Wherever our subjective thinking starts from self-in-
> terest we are blind to the real objective world. Self is a formidable
> enemy in the way of correct summing up of experience to find out
> the laws of the objective world.

What one required from one's thinking, from one's activity
in art as writer or reader, was a shift of emphasis away from that
certainty, that sense of facing an understood world, which character-
ized Marx's early formulation and which characterizes much of the
edifice of orthodox Marxism. One required a more Nietzschean
sense of the world—one that emphasized a change of consciousness,
"a transvaluation of values." For a change of consciousness and
Nietzsche's transvaluation are, I think, the same activity although our
ordinary use of the word *value* disguises this. Values are not merely
held, like a sum of money, by subjects who stand outside them, as if
values could be "held," could be added to an already established self.
Values, in Nietzsche's sense, are a consciousness, a self—as that of
master and slave for example. (And, at the deepest and paradoxical
level, there is that value, or sense of one's self, that allows one to create
or give value—that therefore can create itself, can change itself, making
a constant metamorphosis in which one's self and one's view of the
world are in constant motion.)

To adopt a new, an experimental, stance would be to adopt
for oneself the slogan of the Cultural Revolution in China: "Fight
Self!" It is to look to the art activity—whether as artist or interpreter—for a self-overcoming. Obviously one's vision is formed before

reading a particular work and what we have already come to think will shape what we see; what we see will confirm, at least sometimes, what we think, and so give further evidence for our beliefs. But in reading, as in writing (or any other activity), how much the work changes us as we read it, how much *it reads us,* is the crucial question. When the theory gets to the point that it is not changed by the work, but merely confirmed (when the theory is "perfected') then the theory is rigid, dead; and for a writing or reading that looked for a self-transformation from art it is useless. The theory replaces the work.

This disagreement between theory and art work, between theory and art activity, between the known and the unknown, is the argument between the poet and the philosopher begun in *The Republic* that concludes with the poet's banishment. The philosopher has knowledge of the truth, of the essential nature of things, the eternal forms; the artist is misled by sensuous appearances—he does not know what he is saying and he misleads others. This is the beginning of allegorical criticism. For there are certain texts of the poets, which, though they may mislead the Guardians, are held in too much reverence to be discarded. These texts can be "saved" by giving them an allegorical reading that is in keeping with the truth of philosophy.

The quarrel between the poet and the philosopher is, Plato says, the argument between rationality and the emotions; between the higher and lower faculties ("the element in our nature which is accessible to art and responds to its advances is . . . far from wisdom"); between the common apparent sensuous-material world, and the world of the forms known by the philosopher through his reasoning, known in and through theory. The artist "gratifies that senseless part which cannot distinguish great and small, but regards the same thing as now one, now the other." Reason saves us from this illusory metamorphosis: "But satisfactory means have been found for dispelling these illusions by measuring, counting and weighing. We are no longer at the mercy of apparent differences of size and quantity and weight; the faculty which has done the counting and measuring or weighing takes control instead. And this can only be the work of the calculating or reasoning element in the soul." The argument between poetry and philosophy is the argument between the elect, the instructed, and the masses. The rational, the philosophic, faculty stands above and apart from the masses and instructs them. The artist, who may excite the emotions of the multitude, may do what is pleasing to them, but he is being himself misled by their praise:

> But what of the artist? Has he either knowledge or correct belief? ... Has he even gained a correct belief by being obliged to listen to someone who does know and can tell him how things ought to be represented? No, he has neither.
>
> ·
>
> And yet he will go on with his work, without knowing in what way any of his representations is sound or unsound. He must, apparently, be reproducing only what pleases the taste or wins the approval of the ignorant multitude.

This quarrel is continued in Marxism. The theory takes precedence over the poetry. The artist is always subordinated to the party line. If you are going to write politically—and all writing in Marxism is political writing, all activities are, if rightly understood, political activities—so you are bound, within the theory, to be subordinate to that faculty, "the calculating or reasoning element in the soul," that is, in Lenin's theory, the Party. This faculty is separate from the artistic as it is understood within the theory, and is able to judge which ideas are correct ones. These ideas (later to be worked over by the artistic process, or extracted allegorically from it) are set forth in the theory, judged by the theory, by philosophy, by Marxist science, by something thought of as being outside the artistic process (which becomes, in effect, skill in rendering these ideas).

There is, within the widest compass of Marxist theory, and its interpretation, another idea of art, one put forward by Herbert Marcuse in *Eros and Civilization*. Art, in this work, is presented as autonomous, independent of the political struggle. It is a de-sublimation of the instincts, and so an image of what our activities will be like after the revolution. The aesthetic is independent of politics because it is the goal of political action. "Art," Rilke wrote, "appears, so to speak, as the Weltanschauung of the ultimate goal."

As Marcuse extended and refined this position in his later work (particularly the chapter "Art and Revolution" in *Counterrevolution and Revolt*), art gives expression to the depth-dimension of the personality, the dimension of the instincts, of Eros and Death—instincts that, though the moving forces in history, will never find satisfactory resolution in any social order, will never even show forth truly there. The aesthetic is the goal of the revolution, but it is—within Marcuse's later work (*Counterrevolution and Revolt* and *The Aesthetic Dimension*)—a goal that cannot be reached. The aesthetic is now not activity but image, an image that will always lie ahead of us, though revolutionary success might narrow the distance.

The autonomy of art, its break with the established reality (any reality, even a socialist one) is, Marcuse wrote in *The Aesthetic Dimension*, in and through the aesthetic form. It is the transfiguring power of form that allows the art work to represent sensuously, to show forth the resolution of the instincts that is unachievable in history. By form, by this break with reality, art becomes autonomous of politics. It is the goal of the Party's praxis. Art is of a different metaphysical substance than reality.

But again, in Marcuse's work, the longstanding quarrel between philosophy and poetry is continued, though in a disguised form. The poets are readmitted to the Republic, but in fact they return as philosophers. Only philosophy knows the eternal forms; life is criticized by comparison with the forms. Now, in Marcuse, art represents these unrealizable forms sensuously. Art, for critical theory, is a criticism of life, a goal by which life will always be found wanting, a negation of life.

And the deference of philosophy (or that part of philosophy that has not become art) is only apparent. The art work is mute; although the image is critical by nature, yet because of its necessary muteness (it is a different substance from life) it cannot enter history; the philosopher must mediate the criticism that the image offers, restate the goal in the language of history, show us how it is to be reached, the ways it can enter history, however partially. Even the limits of its entry are set by theory.

"BURNING THE CHRISTMAS GREENS"

There is in the work of Norman O. Brown (as in Blake, or Nietzsche, or in Artaud, or . . . ; but I saw them through Brown's spectacles) another idea of art, or another idea of politics. Art here is neither subservient to the theoretical nor itself a kind of criticism of life. In Brown's later work (*Love's Body* and *Closing Time*), art is not the unreachable goal of politics, nor does the political dictate to the artist; at least not as something that is separate from the artistic acitvity. Instead there is a confusion of realms, a confusion of art and politics. They are the same activity; art is constitutive of the world at every point—if only we had eyes to see. Politics, work, all human culture is symbol formation, is poetry. In his "Reply to Herbert Marcuse," Brown writes, "From politics to poetry. Legislation is not politics, nor philosophy, but poetry. Poetry, art, is not an epiphenomenal reflection of some other (political, economic) realm which is the 'real thing'; nor a sublimation of something else which is the 'real' carnal 'act'. Poetry, art, imagination, the creator spirit is life itself; the real revolutionary power to change the world; and to change the human body." Nietzsche expresses it this way in one of the fragments of *The Will to Power*, "'Life ought to inspire confidence': the task thus imposed is tremendous. To solve it man must be a liar by nature, he must be above all an artist. And he is one: metaphysics, religion, morality, science, all of them only products of his will to art." The will to art is fundamental. There is not some other realm which is the true one; it is not a matter of overcoming repression in order to find the true, the psychoanalytic, the philosophical, the scientific meaning. "When the problem of psychoanalysis becomes not repression but symbolism, when we discover that even if there were no dream censor we should still have symbolism, then personality (soul, ego) becomes not substance, but fiction, representation." All of our works are works of the imagination.

I had begun by looking for a way to read and to write politically; to learn from art, to change myself by it. But what I found was not a new idea of art so much as a new conception of politics; the problem disappeared in its solution. There was not a higher realm of reason, of theory, that must instruct the lower one of the emotions, of the artistic—a higher realm that meant there would never be anything in the art work, the art activity that was not already known. Art itself was the process by which value was created, revolutions made. The political is itself irrational, artistic. And there is no higher realm from which the irrational can be viewed. Art and politics are of the same metaphysical substance. There are only acts of the imagination; there are only poems and the further poems that are comments on them, interpretations of them. This shift moves us away from a world of known activities, known objects named by theory, to a world of metamorphosis, where one creates value by one's activities. What is changed by this value creation, this transvaluation, is not just the world, but oneself, one's vision.

THE REVOLUTIONARY MOMENT

This world of metamorphosis, where the interpreter and the interpretation (his world) are always changing, is the world conveyed to me by the phrase "permanent rovolution." There is no known goal, already embedded within the theory (though the Red Guard speak of being "on the road to revolution"). If there were a "goal," Nietzsche wrote, it would already have been achieved. But there has been a lack of acknowledgement of this goallessness within Marxist theory. The idea of permanent revolution remains a merely rhetorical catch phrase within Marxism, the Marxist equivalent of the word "progress." The idea of permanent revolution has not been allowed to reformulate Marxist theory (nor has Freudian theory been reformulated by the idea of continuous symbolic creation). Marxism, rather than adopting an open-ended experimental stance, has often become an apologetics, a series of rationalizations for why certain historical events didn't occur on schedule, certain revolutions went awry. (During the Cultural Revolution, Mao was more straightforward about this re-visioning of Marxism. He said, "Marxism has many truths, but they all boil down to one truth: It is right to rebel.")

The road of revolution then is that road, that state of consciousness, where the goal is not outside of oneself but is created in fact as one creates oneself. And one could not reflect on one's movements with the same eyes, the same standards with which one had begun, for one would be changed, looking through new eyes.

We make our world as poets, though unconscious ones, as if hypnotized. But even if we recognize this intellectually (that is, *for others*) yet we make our theories, reflect on our poems, as if our reflections were prose, and prose were the true meaning. The second language of reflection deludes itself into thinking it is the master of the first, the poetic one, as if psychoanalysis were cure, as if it could constitute itself outside the constant writing, the constant motion. Philosophy—or psychoanalysis or political theory—which sees the rise and fall of symbols, cannot free itself from the power of symbolism, constitute itself as outside the process by imagining itself at the end. (We think we are moving towards a goal; we watch our motions from the standpoint of that goal, where we have already placed ourselves in imagination, from which we plan the strategy of meeting our selves. But the goal of the revolutionary would change the self; there would be no one there to greet us; we would not know ourselves.) Philosophy, or psychoanalysis, in this mode is like those analysts that Freud wrote of in "Analysis, Terminable and Interminable": "It seems that a number of analysts learn to make use of defensive mechanisms which allow them to divert the implications and demands of analysis from themselves, probably by directing it on to other people—so that they themselves remain as they are, and are able to withdraw from the critical and corrective influences of analysis." But to absorb the critical and corrective influence being spoken of here would be the negation of criticism, the negation of the negation; it would transform psychoanalysis.

"NO IDEAS BUT IN THINGS"

It is all, "a poem containing history," and not, as we first thought, history or political theory or the theory of history, that contains the poems. History, poetry, group psychology, the interpretation of dreams (and nightmares) are branches of the same study: the study of the poetic imagination (a study contained within that imagination). Symptoms—and history as a series of symptoms—are an unconscious, and consequently badly written, poetry. Poetry is a conscious symptom. (Which is not to say that poetry by being "conscious" becomes rational, under the control of the ego as we know it now; rather the poem is what Charles Lamb called "dreaming while awake." (But that is still dreaming.)

Unconscious poets (legislators are the unacknowledged poets of the world) must become conscious ones, ones that recognize that we are interpenetrated with our creations, and that it is by these creations, these necessary angels, that we live; they make us what we are.

One is implicated in things, they share the unconscious, the id. The world as symbol is the world as part of our own psyche. ("Inside the bus," William Carlos Williams writes in *Paterson*, "one sees his thoughts sitting and standing. His/thoughts alight and scatter.")

These ideas opened for me a new path in thinking about politics, and thinking about literature—ways that are, I hope, fruitful in joining the two. Often in the essays that follow I take an artist's attitude toward his material to be a political one (not a disguised manifestation of an already known politics but rather a new creation, an experiment); I take certain ways Joyce tests characters in *Ulysses*, or creates them in *Finnegans Wake*, to be political tests, cultural revolutions; I take certain stances of the artist—the action painters, say—to have important implications for how to think about the problem of work; I look to the poetic and mythological imagination for ecological guidance and I take certain tropes from Williams's poetry—fire and the ground—to be political figures. And in thinking about "politics" (as in my essay on terrorism) I have tried to look to what in me creates society as it is (as in Nietzsche or Freud—where the human psyche is analyzed *en masse*), for we are also poets toward each other.

I must look, for example, to what in me wants a ruling class, wants a spectacle of sacrifice and waste (as I try to do in my essays on *Hamlet* and on terrorism). I try to correct Marx by Freud, and Freud by the poets, and so look to my implication in this order, to the ways that the slave creates his master (as it says in *The Genealogy of Morals*), the way he is in love with his chains, chains that we have made ourselves, "real" chains, that yet are mind-forged manacles, legal fictions, ties that bind.

To say that the ruling class is our collective creation, our projection, or to say that we are implicated in each other unconsciously, act for each other, identify with our priests and victims, does not abolish the ruling class by any means. It is the nature of this sort of thinking that what exists cannot simply be abolished, though it can be re-visioned. (And the idea of abolition—despite the "sublation" of dialectical thinking, whereby the qualities of one stage of development are at the same time taken up by the next stage even as they are "canceled"—is very strong in Marxism.) Poetry is not the criticism of earlier poems, but their interpretation; not repression, but making new, saying it again in a new way, "a new song for a new time." The revolution that we awaited, longed for (or thought we longed for), that we planned (we thought it could be planned as we say a building is planned, as bricks are laid one upon another), is in reality a verse or turning. It is the turnings that make the poem.

HISTORY
IN THE
REVOLUTIONARY
MOMENT

"MEN MADE OUT OF WORDS"

Perhaps there comes a certain time in the life of a nation when it wrestles with an angel to gain its name. In this time a people feel they must find what they will worship and who they are; it is the moment of beginnings, the revolutionary moment. A people then discovers (or recovers—the origin sometimes becomes a second founding) their identity. (It is a time of high talk; in later ages the language seems too unironic, the speech of patriotic pageants.) "The whole race is a poet that writes down/The eccentric propositions of its fate," Wallace Stevens wrote, in "Men Made out of Words." But it is perhaps only in such revolutionary moments that the race, its politicians or its poets, feels this.

The revolutionary moment is intensely poetic and intensely political. For Ireland, Yeats said in his Nobel Prize acceptance speech, this time began with the death of Parnell. "The modern literature of Ireland, and indeed all that stir of thought which prepared for the Anglo-Irish War, began when Parnell fell from power in 1891. A disillusioned and embittered Ireland turned from Parliamentary politics; an event was conceived and the race began, as I think, to be troubled by that long gestation." The revolutionary moment is something that troubles one as if from underground, in the dark, unconsciously, as the word gestation suggests; the nation is something created by a people as a child or dream is created. ("Is there a nation-wide multiform reverie," Yeats asks, "every mind passing through a stream of suggestion, and the streams acting upon one another, no matter how distant the mind, how dumb the lips?") The moment, the time, is, Yeats says, the beginning of modern Irish literature and of the Irish Revolution—they may diverge later, but they were conceived at the same time and take their impetus from the same origin.

This is a rare moment in the life of a nation. It presents its writers with great possibilities: to have their words matter. "These tours [of the Abbey Players]," Yeats wrote, "and Irish songs and novels, when they come from a deeper life than their nineteenth-century predecessors, are taking the place of political speakers, political organizations, in holding together the twenty scattered millions conscious of their Irish blood. The attitude toward life of Irish writers and dramatists at this moment will have historical importance." The artist is contesting something large: the future identity of his country, the shape of the national will, what will be valued, what reviled, "Now and in time to be / Wherever green is worn." The words that we name ourselves in are our propositions about life; they are the words we worship, our necessary angels, momentary deities, tropes that become the substance of life, the music that builds the walls of the city. In this moment a poet's words might become the nation's song, the music it sings to itself about itself, its aspirations; his words might be the very style (rhetorical, exalted, martial, or—unlikely choices—ironic, or comical) in which it will "go forth . . . to encounter reality." "Poets and painters and musicians," Yeats wrote, "are continually making and unmaking mankind."

Ireland was fortunate in its writers. "Few historians," Conor Cruise O'Brien writes in an essay on Yeats's politics, "would challenge Yeats's estimate in his Swedish address of the impact of Parnell's fall and death, or his summary account of a process in which he himself played an important part. His historical sense was keen, as his political sense was also. For he not only saw in retrospect the crucial importance of the death of Parnell. He saw it *at the time*, immediately, and he saw in it his opportunity, and took that opportunity . . . he made Parnell a symbol, almost a god."

This seizing of the occasion was not simple literary opportunism on Yeats's part (as O'Brien sometimes makes it sound), say to gain more readers by making his remarks topical. He wanted his words to matter, and that meant they must come at the right time; there is a strategy, a cunning, to poetry become politics, and politics become poetry. It was not simply opportunism because such times *are* a kind of poetry. Each day brings forth, in Yeats's terms, symbols, prophecies, "Beautiful lofty things: O'Leary's noble head"; or Maude Gonne, "ablaze with politics," "Pallas Athene in that straight back and arrogant head: / All the Olympians; a thing never known again." ("A thing never known again"—I will have more to say on how this phrase embodies Yeats's politics.) Such times, it seems, almost heal the writer's isolation—that distance he often feels between the nature of his role and the world of events, of prose, the political world. Did Yeats make Parnell a symbol, "almost a god," or did he find a symbol, one made by that "multi-form reverie" of the people? The politician is already a symbol, I think; the nation is creating a new world by metaphor. In the revolutionary moment the poet can feel in his own words, in the process that gives birth to those words, the archetypal creative fiat that is then the true nature of both politics and poetry.

A sense of the revolutionary moment is what I think Mandelstam was speaking of when at a similar time in Russian history he wrote: "A heroic era has begun in the life of the word. The word is flesh and bread. It shares the fate of bread and flesh: suffering." Words change their character in the revolutionary moment: words become flesh. Words to us now are the absence of something; if they are used efficaciously they might bring that thing to us as an image, one that speaks to us always by being an image only, of an absence. Or words might command us to perform a certain task, to take some action, to consume some product. Revolutionary words, as Mandelstam conceived them, do not bring things to us: they are bodies, that is to say, speaking them makes *us*, or changes us. Such words are what Vico described as the activity of the first men; man makes himself by making his poetry, by making his gods, and his gods are poetic creations, so he is a poetic creation. In such words we re-form ourselves and so re-make our world.

During the revolutionary moment, as Mandelstam reveals it to us, poetry and politics have become a new kind of activity. The word has become a kind of deed: it changes the self. And the deed has become a word. We can feel that we are a made thing in such times; that our body too is our joint creation, that our hungers are therefore also meaningful hungers, symbolic creations, spiritual needs (spiritual because the creation is as if from outside). Work, the objects of the world that we make and that fulfill such needs, is therefore also a kind of word. Mandelstam wrote "Apples, bread, potatoes—from now on satisfy not only physical but spiritual hungers as well. A Christian does not know only physical hunger alone, only spiritual food. For him the word is flesh, and common bread is merriment and mystery." Politics and poetry and work are kinds of writing (words are flesh and bread, flesh and bread are words). Or as Yeats put a thought similar to Mandelstam's, though his sense of a symbol is different, it is "as though some ballad-singer had sung it all."

Joyce also describes the beginning of this moment, this struggle with an angel in which both a nation and its artists find a vocation, in *A Portrait of the Artist as a Young Man*:

> John Alphonsus Mulrennan has just returned from the west of Ireland. European and Asiatic papers please copy. He told us he met an old man there in a mountain cabin. Old man had red eyes and short pipe. Old man spoke Irish. Mulrennan spoke Irish. Then old man and Mulrennan spoke English. Mulrennan spoke to him about universe and stars. Old man sat, listened, smoked, spat. Then said:
> —Ah, there must be terrible queer creatures at the latter end of the world.—
> I fear him. I fear his redrimmed horny eyes. It is with him I must struggle all through this night till day come, till he or I lie dead, gripping him by the sinewy throat till . . . Till what? Till he yield to me? No. I mean him no harm.

And Stephen leaves Ireland and the novel, speaking of what is, in some way, being contested between himself and the old man: "I go to encounter for the millionth time the reality of experience and to forge in the smithy of my soul the uncreated conscience of my race."

It is crucial to this moment, as Joyce perceived it, and as he perceived himself perceiving it, that it is not with the English but with the Irish themselves that he must wrestle for his name, and for theirs, the race's as yet fortunately uncreated conscience.

It is with the Irish he must struggle; that is, with himself. Politics—in the sense of flattery, or of the kind of rallying and effective insult that Yeats was so expert at, where one speaks of one's fierce disappointment in the fallen state of a great and noble people—was closed to him; he is, from that sort of politics, an exile. (Though he might be the creator of a new political sense it will be from exile, from underground.)

The old man of this passage is alien, almost assimilated to nature by the simple will-less (and ironic) rhythm of the verbs that describes him. ("Old man sat, listened, smoked, spat.") He is red-rimmed eyes, a demon—a figure from, or *for*, the unconscious. There is, of course, irony throughout this passage; Joyce will at first find his vocation in irony and within the self-perception that is part of the ironic stance; that will be essential to what he will offer in *Ulysses*. Here there is no exact target on Stephen's part for his irony; himself, Mulrennan, the old man are all touched by it (they live "where motley is worn"). Most strongly, it is the provincialism of Dublin that is mocked, their way of seeing too large a significance, too heroic a meaning ("European and Asiatic papers please copy") in their own acts, and especially in their contact with the folk. (To see meaning is, however, the vocation of the artist, which may account for the irony going out of place here.) The old man and Mulrennan exchange phrases in Irish, as if they were only signals ("I'm a peasant . . . I'm from the Gaelic League"), for they quickly switch to English. The old man, by this apparent cooperation in the signaling, becomes, I think, an ironic, self-ironic figure (there are no ironic peasants within the Irish folk movement, only sly ones). Stephen cannot simply condescend to the old man, though, for he is Stephen's opponent. Interesting that it is the peasant who is Joyce's enemy here, and not the Dubliners who will be his actual opponents in the struggle to publish his books in Ireland. It is with the old man that Joyce must wrestle, although he means him no harm, doesn't want him to yield—though the question of what he does want ("Till what?" Stephen asks), how long this struggle must go on, and what its exact nature will be, resonate throughout Joyce's career, finding, I think, an unexpected answer in *Finnegans Wake*.

Stephen and the old man will struggle; but Stephen means

him no harm. He has, in fact, as he tells us at the end of the novel, something to offer the old man: articulation. He will create the as yet uncreated conscience of his race. The old man on the other hand offers Stephen something (as Parnell's death offered Yeats), the opportunity to provide that conscience; the old man offers him a vocation.

Yeats, also took part in this struggle, offering the Irish a version of themselves to behold and so become. His was an Ireland of the past, of folk tales and stately mansions. (They were, Yeats indicates, in some way the same world; both the aristocracy and the peasants shared a habit of thought, an ordered tradition, a world of "intuitive knowledge.") Yeats did not wish to wrestle with the old man, but rather to take down his remarks about the queer creatures at the end of the world and make them into verse. "I thought that all art should be a Centaur finding in the popular lore its back and its strong legs . . . We had in Ireland imaginative stories, which the uneducated classes knew and even sang, and might we not make those stories current among the educated classes . . . and at last, it might be, so deepen the political passion of the nation, that all, artist and poet, craftsman and day-labourer would accept a common design?" The peasants are, for the poet, opportunity; as he told a young Irish poet, one should write about Irish legends and places: "It helps originality and makes one's verses sincere and gives one less numerous competitors."

Yeats's style underwent a striking transformation.

In a diary note dated Christmas, 1912, [Richard Ellmann writes, in *Yeats, the Man and the Mask*] he stated succinctly his present theory of art:

First Principles

Not to find one's art by the analysis of language or amid the circumstances of dreams but to live a passionate life, and to express the emotions that find one thus in simple rhythmical language. . . .

To see how far he had come [Ellmann continues] we may set against this manifesto one he had made thirteen years before in an essay called "The Autumn of the Flesh." It is almost the exact contrary:

I see, indeed, in the arts of every country those faint lights and faint colours and faint outlines and faint energies which many call "the decadence," and which I . . . prefer to call the autumn of the flesh . . . . Man has wooed and won the world, and has fallen weary, and not, I think, for a time, but with a weariness that will not end until the last autumn, when the shares shall be blown away like withered leaves.

But what is equally striking in Yeats's poetry is not what changes, but what remains the same. The thematic tone of much of his greatest poetry, the tonality of ideas, attitudes, and postures taken, remain, I think, consistent throughout his work. That tone, which he describes in "The Autumn of the Flesh," "Man has wooed and won the world, and has fallen weary, and not, I think, for a time . . ." is a tone that one would describe as elegiac: "The elegaic presents a heroism unspoiled by irony, a diffused resigned menlancholy sense of the passing of time, the old order changing and yielding to a new one."

> The nineteenth autumn has come upon me
> Since I first made my count;
> I saw, before I had well finished,
> All suddenly mount
> And scatter wheeling in great broken rings
> Upon their clamorous wings.
>
> I have looked upon those brilliant creatures,
> And now my heart is sore.
> All's changed since I, hearing at twilight,
> The first time on this shore,
> The bell beat of their wings above my head,
> Trod with a lighter tread.

Autumn is the season in this poem, this elegy, "The Wild Swans at Coole," the characteristic time for Yeats's poetry. (There was first moment, when he trod with a lighter tread; but this time though remembered, is almost always absent from direct presentation in the poem itself.) Autumn is the characteristic time for Yeats's apprehension of the revolutionary moment, an always failing return to origin. It is close of day; the end of the cycle for Yeats (Celtic twilight, or "Cultic twalette," as Joyce called it). What is richest and most alive, most lovely, least anxious, most vivid, most present, is, for Yeats, in the past, recaptured only in memory, speaking to us as one of the things of memory might. "The Wild Swans at Coole" is calm and reflective, regretful, detached from present time, elegiac; the characteristic phrase, I think, is "All's changed . . ."

"All's changed . . . " The phrase recurs when Yeats revisits "Coole Park and Ballyee, 1931":

> A spot whereon the founders lived and died
> Seemed once more dear than life; ancestral trees,
> Or gardens rich in memory glorified
> Marriages, alliances and families,
> And every bride's ambition satisfied.
> Where fashion or mere fantasy decrees
> We shift about—all that great glory spent—
> Like some poor Arab tribesman and his tent.
>
> We were the last romantics—chose for theme
> Traditional sanctity and loveliness;
> Whatever's written in what poets name
> The book of the people; whatever most can bless
> The mind of man or elevate a rhyme;
> But all is changed, that high horse riderless,
> Though mounted in that saddle Homer rode
> Where the swan drifts upon a darkening flood.

"But all is changed . . . " The poet here in this later poem is as masterfully elegiac, but less unperturbedly so. Now there is a "darkening flood" to be feared, or "blood-dimmed tide" (as he named it in "The Second Coming," a somewhat earlier poem). A new note haunts Yeats's poetry, near a kind of terror; yet the tone remains elegiac (and it is one facet of his art to be true to both these feelings). A consciousness, a style of consciousness, one that does not shift about, is going under, being drowned; but this going under (I think we can feel in the last verse) is not only defeat, it is also exaltation, for the dying world is most beautiful as it is most utterly lost; and the poet is at the peak of his powers because he has remembered it, has sung it even in the face of this catastrophe that will overwhelm him, will overwhelm poetry. For to face the end, the apocalypse, the darkening flood, is also to feel most strongly *oneself* in the very bitterness of the last moment.

And this elegiac exultation was characteristic too of a certain style of politics of the time, one that saw itself as facing the decline of the West, as facing the barbarian hordes of the East, the rising tide of the masses, that knew itself as aristocratic because of its distance from this "mass of interchangeable people." Its time was also autumn. And this is the time that Yeats himself evokes for this politics, in discussing his feelings for fascism: "Italy, Poland, Germany, then perhaps Ireland. Doubtless I shall hate it (though not so much as I hate Irish democracy) but it is September and we must not behave like the gay young sparks of May or June."

Yeats looked to the past because, first of all, it was in the past that a certain myth (but it was not yet "myth," it was, he thought, a lived reality) and way of life were in congruence. The objects men lived among in this lost world were not dead things, but spoke to us of ourselves as symbols do. It was a "total world," an ordered world, a world "instinct with piety" (as Proust called his personal lost world) in which things were unalien to us, all a single indivisible whole. It is this world that Yeats holds before himself, this world that he meditates on in time of civil war—it is disappearing, always disappearing, even as it is named—this world, our ancestral home:

> Surely among a rich man's flowering lawns,
> Amid the rustle of his planted hills,
> Life overflows without ambitious pains;
> And rains down life until the basin spills,
> And mounts more dizzy high the more it rains
> As though to choose whatever shape it wills
> And never stoop to a mechanical
> Or servile shape, at others' beck and call.

This world, where Being is present to us, and "Life over-flows without ambitious pains; / And rains down life until the basin spills" is the inherited glory of the rich. But the world of industry, of mechanical shapes, has caused it to go under, has turned it to a world of fragments, where ambitious men, seeking only their own profit, rule. A symbol is an emergence from this lost world: it is the voice of the dead. "The aura we feel in a symbol," Denis Donoghue writes of Yeats's symbolism, "is the presence of the supernatural in the natural; the souls of the dead are understood as living in places which are sacred because of that residence . . . Belief in reincarnation is endorsed by assent to tradition; Symbolism is the hermeneutics of that faith." It is the race itself that through the Great Mind gives us symbols. Symbols are for Yeats the creative words of the race, but the race of the past, the dead. "The dead living in their memories are, I am persuaded, the source of all that we call instinct, and it is their love and their desire, all unknowing, that makes us drive beyond our reason, or in defiance of our interest it may be." The emergence of the symbol is no longer the creative work of the revolutionary moment, but the imposition of the past; the nation—essentially passive (symbols aren't made, but received)—only calls up the voices of the dead, brings blood to their ghosts. The dead will occupy them, and by this occupation, the visionary moment turns the present into the past. This is emblematized by Yeats's speech at the banquet for Wolf Tone in 1893: "We are building up a nation which shall be moved by noble purposes and to noble ends. A day will come for her, though not perhaps, in our day. There is an old story that tells how sometimes when a ship is beaten by storm and almost upon the rocks, a mysterious figure appears and lays its hand upon the tiller. It is Mannanan, the son of Lir, the old god of the waters. So it is with nations, a flaming hand is laid suddenly upon the tiller." The people's activity is not creation, but helplessness that requires the god's intervention. The present is invaded by the past.

To recapture the lost world in the visionary moment is the poet's work; it is to bring two lenses together (self and antiself) inside the Self (the only place they can be brought together now; the heart is moved "but to the heart's discovery of itself"), to a focus where mythic consciousness and reality seem to meet for a moment, and the world becomes our home, a place of self-contained satisfaction and mastery. "Yet I am certain," Yeats wrote, "that there was something in myself compelling me to attempt creation of an art as separate from everything heterogeneous and casual, all character and circumstance, as some Herodiade of our theater, dancing seemingly alone in her narrow moving circle." This world—all that is heterogeneous and casual—falls away from the dancer, within the circle of her self. "And all about lives but in mine own / Image, the idolatrous mirror of my pride, / Mirroring this Herodiade diamond eyed."

From this self-contemplation the dancer (the poet) may give

forth a gesure; a gesture that she will not herself—outside the circle
of her dance—understand:

> What matter that you understood no word!
> Doubtless I spoke or sang what I had heard
> In broken sentences. My soul had found
> All happiness in its own cause or ground
> Godhead on Godhead in sexual spasm begot
> Godhead. Some shadow fell. My soul forgot
> Those amourous cries that out of quiet come
> And must the common round of day resume.

The gesture of the poet or the dancer is to us an elegy— the
visionary moment falls away, back into a past that leaves the present
bitter, empty, longing. The visionary moment contains within itself
a mourning.

Yeats looks for the lost world everywhere, but finds it only
in fragments, in broken sentences, moments of memory and prophecy
(that are, we shall see, the same sorts of fragments). "I desire a
mysterious art," Yeats wrote, "always reminding and half-reminding
those who understand it of dearly loved things, doing its work by
suggestion, not by direct statement, a complexity of rhythm, colour,
gesture, not space-pervading like the intellect but a memory and a
prophecy: a mode of drama . . ." The dearly loved things are always
absent.

The emergence of the symbol, of the prophecy, is for Yeats,
the destruction of the present moment; the self is moved into a
future time in which he looks back on the destruction of what is
(though not the destruction of the observing self); the symbolic
prophecy makes of this world a dying world, a fit subject for elegy.
The world enters the poem only as a figure of the past. And again
this prophecy of destruction, of time closing, is not only an elegy,
but an exultation, the exultation of being present at one's own
funeral, singing one's own death, and so surviving it, savoring it (for
it is within the imagination). The Yeatsian world is one of "brooding
memory and dangerous hope," but the dangerous hope turns all
into the realm of memory. All is possessed in loss, contained within
the self, even one's own death.

This elegiac tone, one might think, would cut one off from contesting the nation's political future, the nation's identity. However, it is close to the ideologies of both left and right that have dominated the political thought of this century, for we are nostalgic for a total world, a world of order, completeness, unity of Being. Recurrently nations have wished to imagine the future in the image of a lost past, a reconciliation with the dead, an atonement; a future in which our souls will be occupied by immortal ancestral voices; one in which our lost father speaks to us directly.

This desire for a congruence of myth and reality, for an enclosed and speaking world, is not only of the right. There are also elegies of the left. In Walter Benjamin's remarks on the aura a similar elegiac longing can be heard. "Aura," Benjamin writes, is "the single unrepeatable experience of distance, no matter how close it may be. While resting on a summer afternoon, to follow the outline of a mountain against the horizon, or of a branch that casts its shadow on the viewer, means to breath the aura of the mountain, of the branch." This aura is the Yeatsian moment when the branch becomes mystery, becomes symbol. Commenting on this passage of Benjamin's, Fredric Jameson writes, "Aura is . . . a mysterious wholeness of objects become visible . . . And where the broken objects of allegory represented a thing world of destructive forces in which human autonomy was drowned, the objects of aura stand perhaps as the setting of a kind of Utopia, . . . not shorn of the past, but having absorbed it, a kind of plentitude of existence in a world of things, if only for the briefest instant. Yet this Utopian component of Benjamin's thought, put to flight as it is by the mechanized present of history, is available to the thinker only in a simpler cultural past." Here, in the Marxist Benjamin, are themes and presences very close to Yeats's: an elegy, a nostalgia for a world of speaking things, a world now drowned in the mechanical and servile shapes of the industrial present.

This longing, the emphasis on memory, can also be found in Herbert Marcuse's work. The difference—and perhaps it is a politically crucial one—is that the time of plentitude of being. of union with the world, is for Marcuse not a historical moment in the past, but a phase in the life of every infant, and, in *Eros and Civilization*, the image of a possible future.

Elegy—longing for the past—does not seal one off from the world of politics either on the right or the left. Yeats, more than all but a few of the writers of his time, (Pound and Brecht come to mind, though each had only partially the chance Yeats had to matter most directly) took the largest risks, led his deepest life in public— even when his poetry complained of the savage effects of too much public life. It was his genius, his generosity in the use of himself, to find the public within the private, to find that place (a place clearly of bad dreams, terrifying apparitions, disgust, regret, extremities of hope and savagery) within oneself where one's quarrel with the world, and one's quarrel with oneself can truly be apprehended as the same skirmishing; and out of this apprehension he constructed some of the enduring political prophecies for his (our, any) time; mistakes worth wondering at, places where the road comes recurrently, and forks off, and history goes wandering in error again.

"All's changed . . . " The phrase finds its greatest exaltation in "Easter, 1916." The revolution, the political identity of the nation, will not come from the stately mansions, but from the little streets (and their leaders) as they are hurled upon the great. Yeats turns here to the task of ennobling those little men, of taking them up into his imagination, his rhetoric, his traditional grand manner.

> I have met them at close of day
> Coming with vivid faces
> From counter or desk among grey
> Eighteenth-century houses.
> I have passed with a nod of the head
> Or polite meaningless words,
> And thought before I had done
> Of a mocking tale or a gibe
> To please a companion
> Around the fire at the club,
> Being certain that they and I
> But lived where motley is worn:
> All changed, changed utterly:
> A terrible beauty is born.
> . . . .
> This other man I had dreamed
> A drunken, vainglorious lout.
> He had done most bitter wrong
> To some who are near my heart,

Yet I number him in the song;
He, too, has resigned his part
In the casual comedy;
He, too, has been changed in his turn,
Transformed utterly:
A terrible beauty is born.
. . . .

We know their dream; enough
To know they dreamed and are dead;
And what if excess of love
Bewildered them till they died?
I write it out in a verse—
MacDonagh and MacBride
And Connolly and Pearse
Now and in time to be,
Wherever green is worn,
Are changed, changed utterly:
A terrible beauty is born.

Yeats takes figures of the Easter Rebellion up into his imagination, numbering them in his verse. But this also means taking them up into the past, the past that is the very substance of Yeats's language, his high style and his poetic method. In this poem, elegy and epic are as close to being one as—in this world—they can be. The figures of the rising are no longer comic; they have ceased to play a part; Being and becoming, Being and appearance are one in the dignity of death ("Let be be finale of seem"). The epic wholeness in this fallen world can be regained only in memory, after the event, in death, as story. The figures of "Easter, 1916" are exalted in the poem, and yet the very substance of the poem reveals that its politics are those of elegy, and of an activism that can only have as its end, elegy, which is to say, death. The poem insists that, regretfully, there is something about politics and about fanaticism (they were for Yeats—not always figuratively—the same) that makes one unliving, that "too long a [political] sacrifice can make a stone of the heart." ("The revolutionary," Nechayev said, "is a doomed man." He is one who imagines himself already dead.) But the poem itself shows that it is sacrifice, not metaphorical but actual physical sacrifice that is ennobling. The figures are beautiful not in victory, but in defeat; the exultation is felt in tragedy, in death. And Yeats, when he came to write for an Irish Fascist movement ("Three Songs to the Same Tune"), stresses throughout the beauty of dying for a cause:

> "Money is good and a girl might be better,
> No matter what happens and who takes the fall,
> But a good strong cause"—the rope gave a jerk there,
> No more sang he, for his throat was too small;
> But he kicked before he died,
> He did it out of pride.

"All's changed..." The phrase in "Easter, 1916" seems at first to have reversed its meaning; the men are changed into something beautiful; it is not a lament over the fallen state of the world. But the figures are transformed, their terrible beauty released, made actual, only by their joining the lost world at the moment of their dying. In an elegy, Northrop Frye says, the subject of the poem is "idealized and exalted into a nature spirit or dying god." Possession by the dead has become death itself; dying they are united with the god. The poet survives to number them in his verse, for now that they are lost they are poetic figures. The poet survives: elegy is the song of a survivor.

THE BLACK DOT

As Yeats's style is exalted, Joyce's, in *Ulysses*, is parodic. Yeats's style draws on the past of intuitive knowledge, of traditional songs and traditional texts; Joyce's style—his identity—includes the slang, the colloquial, the polyglot, the language of the little streets, the language not of folk tales but of the music hall. *Ulysses* includes the mocking tales and gibes that Yeats might have made up to please a companion at the club, and includes also the gibes Joyce made up about Yeats and that companion. The men at the bar in the "Cyclops" chapter of *Ulysses*, Lenehan, Bob Doran, Alf Bergin, and the Citizen, could have been like the drunken vainglorious lout who "resigned his part" and died in the Easter Rising. But in Joyce's world he still lives where motley is worn, nor would dying have taken him out of that world. Every pretension towards a martial heroism is mocked by the writing of the chapter. The heroic is comic lists, overblown descriptions, pretentious bombast.

The styles in which heroism is described, in which it becomes heroism (and so comes to form the consciousness of future generations) are dealt with by Joyce, parodied, emptied of meaning, destroyed.

These styles—and the events they claim to represent, and the meanings they try to give these events—are lies. True heroism, in this novel, is elsewhere. More humane, it has more self-knowledge than an old style hero can bear, is modest, and somewhat comical. It does wear motley, and that continually, never resigning its part—nor is it clear what resigning one's part would mean in *Ulysses*. (Dying? Pawning one's furniture?) It is in the nature of one's identity in this novel to be taken up into other larger identities, rhetorical systems; one can play different parts, but not give up playing parts. The life of the hero in *Ulysses* is a series of surreal music hall turns. Here the avatar of heroism—the myth of Odysseus is another of the larger systems that take up the characters—is Leopold Bloom, commercial traveler, wanderer, the little fellow from a little street. Like Chaplin, he is one who lacks the ability to impose on others, the rhetoric to impress them. And so, as with Chaplin's ineffective and confused comic gestures, his plans at cross purposes, Bloom's speeches are self-divided, not quite articulate—opportunities for others to mock him.

> —Persecution says he, all the history of the world is full of it. Perpetuating national hatred among nations.
> —But do you know what a nation means? says John Wyse.
> —Yes, says Bloom.
> —What is it? says John Wyse.
> —A nation? says Bloom. A nation is the same people living in the same place.
> —By God, then, says Ned, laughing, if that's so I'm a nation for I'm living in the same place for the past five years.
> So of course everyone had a laugh at Bloom and says he, trying to muck out of it:
> —Or also living in different places.
> —That covers my case, says Joe.
> —What is your nation if I may ask, says the citizen.
> —Ireland says Bloom. I was born here, Ireland.

"So of course everyone had a laugh at Bloom . . ." Putting on his hat Bloom had knocked over a vase; picking up the vase he has lost his hat again. The exchange is a music hall turn—Mr. Bones and the Interlocuter—and yet, despite his playing Mr. Bones, it is Bloom who is clearly sane here. For every imposition of rhetoric—as the word nation itself—is hollow. Nation is not the saving Word we are in search of throughout *Ulysses*; it is what Erik Erikson calls a "pseudo-identity." Bloom's inability to define it, which allows for the comedy, is not a lack in him, but in it. His final inarticulation: "Ireland ... I was born here, Ireland," shows, in its simplicity, its reduction, its lack of ornament, the bedrock that underlies the Joycean playfulness in the book, the man behind the mask, Bloom as Cordelia, almost silent, Charlie offering a dusty bouquet.

> —And I belong to a race too, says Bloom, that is hated and persecuted. Also now. This very moment. This very instant.
>
> Gob, he near burnt his fingers with the butt of his old cigar.
>
> —Robbed, says he. Plundered. Insulted. Persecuted. Taking what belongs to us by right. At this very moment, says he, putting up his fist, sold by auction off in Morocco like slaves or cattles.
>
> —Are you talking about the new Jerusalem? says the citizen.
>
> —I'm talking about injustice, says Bloom.
>
> —Right, says John Wyse. Stand up to it then with force like men.
>
> That's an almanac picture for you. Mark for a softnosed bullet. Old lardyface standing up to the business end of a gun. Gob, he'd adorn a sweepingbrush, so he would, if he only had a nurse's apron on him. And then he collapses all of a sudden, twisting around all the opposite, as limp as a wet rag.
>
> —But it's no use, says he. Force, hatred, history, all that. That's not life for men and women, insult and hatred. And everyone knows that it's the very opposite of that that is really life.
>
> —What? says Alf.
>
> —Love, says Bloom. I mean the opposite of hatred.

For Yeats there is a separation between the ancestral home and the bars where the masses drink, a separation between the heroic fighter of "Easter, 1916" and the drunken lout he was before his transformation; a separation then between the language of the town ("Old lardyface standing up to the business end of a gun. Gob, he'd adorn a sweepingbrush, so he would, if he only had a nurse's apron on him") and the martial music of his political poetry:

> The soldier takes pride in saluting his Captain,
> The devotee proffers a knee to his Lord,
> Some back a mare thrown from a thoroughbred,
> Troy backed its Helen; Troy died and adored;
> Great nations blossom above;
> A slave bows down to a slave.

Near the end of his life Yeats reminds himself that there is another truth. In the "The Circus Animals' Desertion," there is no longer a simple opposition between high and low, between the high style, high images, and the common, the rubbish heap.

> Those masterful images because complete
> Grew in pure mind, but out of what began?
> A mound of refuse or the sweepings of a street,
> Old kettles, old bottles, and a broken can,
> Old iron, old bones, old rags, that raving slut
> Who keeps the till. Now that my ladder's gone,
> I must lie down where all the ladders start,
> In the foul rag-and-bone shop of the heart.

Yeats's reconciliation is partial, provisional; there is a strong formal irony at work here which modifies his assertions. The poem is a stripping bare in which the emperor does not reveal his clothes to be illusory, but, like a king going to his execution, strips off his beautiful garments one by one, holding each of them up for our admiration, savoring it the more by contrast with the rags that await him; again, things are valued most at the point of loss. The poem is not iconoclastic, not a debunking, but a walk to the gallows—and a walk to the gallows does not demythify the king; rude hands may break into the Lord's anointed temple, but the confrontation between the sacred and the profane does not call into question the sacredness that is being lost, the ritual that is being fulfilled. The poet puts behind him worldly wordy glory, but it is the glory that pervades the early stanzas that has his love. The funeral march concludes in the foul rag-and-bone shop of the heart, but the poet is not shown taking up residence there, only announcing that he is forced to. Of course, for purposes of contrast with his previous state, matters must be made very bad in the rag-and-bone shop. The raving slut who keeps the till (to continue his personification) would not lie down in that foulness (she probably doesn't think of herself as a raving slut either). Only a nobleman, proving how far he has fallen, heaping shame on the world by heaping shame on himself, lies down in a gutter. His abasement is then only another image of his pride. The poem is an elegy, mourning a loss—a loss still believed, even if ostensibly denied. The Yeatsian personality, the Yeatsian style, like the line of his poetry, is here smooth, uncontrite, unbroken. (The giddy elevation of a poem like "High Talk" is a far more convincing instance of the personality coming out of itself, its being transformed by metaphor.)

Joyce is more at home in the rubbish heap (in *Finnegans Wake*, it is the very image of history). There is, in the "Cyclops" chapter, a far more rapid alternation between the high and the low. (It is still an alternation, a rapid jazz. Joyce does not yet—nor could he, given the suppositions of *Ulysses*—capture the two in one; for that would destroy the integrity of the self that I think *Ulysses*'s form finally supports.) The cigar that Bloom holds becomes the spike that menaces the Cyclops's eye. A handkerchief is the treasured artifact of the nation. Bloom himself undergoes metamorphosis, holding a broom, facing a gun, pushing a broom, becoming a nurse, twisting around all the opposite, as limp as a wet rag. The question is raised by the rapidity of these alternations, whether these two realms—martial music (such as it is in this book), the nation, sacrifice, and the bar, the cigar, the "Red Bank Oyster," the smell, the foul rag-and-bone shop of bodily facts—are in fact as opposite as Yeats by his tone implies, even as Yeats overtly denies their opposition. (The very strength of Yeats's assertion is a sign of the distance—for there is still something to be mortified by the assertion.) Joyce, like Chaplin, is debunking, iconoclastic; one can understand why so sensitive a reader as E. M. Forster felt that Joyce was "covering the world with mud."

Joyce's irony does not, I think, quite cover the whole world with mud. Bloom himself remains, if not uncovered, unaffected by the mud. There is in him something that could be mortified, could be lost, and is not. It is of the novel's essence that though we feel

Bloom to be more real than many of the other characters, more sincere, more good hearted, yet that truth, like Luther's faith, may be nearly unexpressible in the fallen words that this fallen world offers. When Bloom speaks, "—Love, says Bloom. I mean the opposite of hatred," he has to work with only the most clownish of clichés, or the simplest of statements, words that mean little or do not mean what he wishes, words that Joyce himself must in fairness proceed to parody. (For the word *love* is not far from the word *nation*.) "Love loves to love love. Nurse loves the new chemist. Constable 14 A loves Mary Kelly . . . Jumbo, the elephant, loves Alice, the elephant . . . You love a certain person. And this person loves that other person because everybody loves somebody but God loves everybody."

Bloom's affirmation—"Love . . . I mean the opposite of hatred"—is as ridiculous as any other remark in the world, or if less so, it is because it is more humble, more open in its foolishness. Bloom's language is turned by Joyce into the language of smile buttons and Hallmark greeting cards. It is as if the parody were a test to see if the sentiment will survive the treatment. For the only words we have have been degraded; they do not match something we call our feelings, something finer than the counters we have to express them with. The truth must survive under its opposite; incognito, it must go forth in the language of lies. So, too, the assumption is that Bloom's consciousness, though degraded by what it has to work with, is also something more sincere, something untouched. This is what makes Bloom heroic: an outsider, at home nowhere, he makes do.

The language of lies that Bloom must survive in is what is usually called propaganda. *Ulysses* is a compendium of this language: newspapers, handbills, the advertising sandwich board man, popular novels, magazines—all are forces, systems, languages that are outside the ego's control. And they are all forces that impinge on Bloom's consciousness. About propaganda John Berger has written that it "preserves within people outdated structures of feeling and thinking whilst forcing new experiences upon them. It transforms them into puppets. The only purpose of such propaganda is to make people deny and then abandon the selves which otherwise they might create." Propaganda makes a world that is not the world, or at least not, Berger is saying, the world that could be. Propaganda, in these terms, cannot undo those dissatisfactions, those contradictions, that made it a necessity in the first place; repression is continual; a sense of living in two worlds at once quite common; schizophrenia an everyday occurrence.

Propaganda is a lie in the head that one confuses for one's own voice; one refrains from "creating the uncreated conscience of our race" (thus the necessity for silence for Stephen to do his work at the end of *A Portrait*). If a poem is creative, a naming that reshapes the world and the self, propaganda draws on the resources of poetry in the name of a kind of social ego strength. It looks for symbolic manipulations that will allow for the maintenance of the self as it is.

Voices: this is Bloom as Gerty McDowell forms him for herself (and we overhear):

> And while she gazed her heart went pitapat. Yes, it was her he was looking at and there was meaning in his look. His eyes burned into her as though they would search her through and through, read her very soul. Wonderful eyes they were, superbly expressive, but could you trust them . . . ? She could see at once by his dark eyes and his pale intellectual face that he was a foreigner the image of the photo she had of Martin Harvey, the matinée idol . . . Here was that of which she had so often dreamed.

Gerty dreams of Bloom, or daydreams, but the dream is not her own. It is a dream manufactured for her by *Lady's Pictorial,* the makers of Martin Harvey, matinée idol. There is in this novel a boundary drawn between those who write for such magazines, and those who read them. Gerty, one assumes, is being imposed on. This boundary grows very thin when we remember the "smart operators" whom we met at the newspaper office, and thinner still when Bloom imagines writing one of those stories. But the boundary is finally impermeable, for it is signified by the distinction between the readers of *Lady's Pictorial,* and the readers of *Ulysses.* It is assumed, I think, that *Ulysses* does not impose on us. Using alienation affects to distance us from the characters, it is a book that requires a keen critical intelligence for its navigation; we are encouraged by its technique to come backstage, to watch its construction. The readers of *Ulysses* can laugh at the readers of *Lady's Pictorial,* though with that comforting sense that, well, we are really not so different from them—an admission we feel comfortable in making because irony allows us to feel that we are freely making the admission; it is in our power to make it; we are not imposed on.

Gerty repeats the voices more naively than we would. Although the scene is interrupted—by her voice, conversations with friends, thoughts that move a little distance from stylization—still the parody is fairly broad. The character is turned into a somewhat crudely drawn cartoon. But the assumption of such a drawing is still, I think, that there is a human form underneath, and that the readers of the parody can see it, that they know what is being deformed and reformed here. The truth is being revealed to us by a manipulation of the language of lies. ("It's the very opposite of that that is really life," Bloom says.) There is, it is assumed, a real voice, separate from the imposed voices; one in the characters, one in the reader, one in the author, and each can be heard and distinguished from all other voices, if only as an absent overtone.

Bloom is of course in no way innocent in the exchange with Gerty. Not only is his masturbation juxtaposed to Gerty's romantic description, but Bloom is far more complicitous than that: He thinks of working up a little story about the whole incident: "*The Mystery Man on the Beach,* prize titbit story by Mr. Leopold Bloom. Payment at the rate of one guinea per column." This then would be a story made up of other stories, retold in the language that ravished Gerty's mind, brought about the hiking up of her skirts that gave birth to a new story. Given the premise of minds imposing on each other this is the only kind of truly imagined ravishment that occurs in the scene.

In the later chapters of *Ulysses* the consciousnesses of Bloom and Stephen seem almost to disappear under the weight of the impositions they are subjected to. Their characters are taken up, represented as parts of other modes of consciousness; they are modalities of other modes; Gerty's lady magazine consciousness, the mock heroic, the history of English prose. In "Circe" the infantile wishes, the perversities, the fantasies, the disowned parts of the mind are exhibited and parodied. But this element of parody is a regression in the service of the ego; someone (an established self, an established set of values) is playing; a strong ego is one that gains from play.

Bloom is taken up into his fantasies (ones we know were close to Joyce's own) and suffers their acting out. He is for the moment altogether the masochist who licks Bella's boots, as in the previous chapter he had seemed no more than a sign in the prose of Sir Thomas Malory. The dissolution of Bloom's character makes him appear as almost only a function of different languages, different signifying systems, as they meet the resistance of his consciousness, his intention. Bloom changes, and changes again, twisting about like a wet rag, repeating the clichés of his time, moving from part to part, language to language. Yet "longest way round is shortest way home" as it says in the "Ithaca" chapter. And there is in *Ulysses* a home to go to; an ineluctable self that one returns to after one's wanderings, one's mask play; after all the unravelings, Bloom returns to his identity. As Stephen says, "If Socrates leaves his house today he will find the sage on his doorstep. If Judas go forth tonight it is to Judas his steps will tend . . . We walk through ourselves meeting robbers, ghosts, giants, old men, young men, wives, widows, brothers-in-love. But always meeting ourselves." The parodies, the contesting styles of the novel, war as if for Bloom's soul, testing whether or not his identity, his single indivisible self, his way of ordering the world, of finding and making value, can survive. And he does survive, in that we feel none of the styles contains Bloom quite (the way Gerty is nearly contained). There is, we are to feel, an irreducible core to Bloom, symbolized by the round thick black dot that ends the "Ithaca" chapter. Bloom's self is more than any voice can contain, more noble than any parody can diminish; it is the center that allows for crude outlinings, for the center is still recogni able and is also the vantage point that allows for parody, the settled sense of self, ego strength. As S. L. Goldberg writes:

> In "Circe" his nature prevents him from being swallowed up in any simplification of his essential humanity. He is neither social Messiah, nor social martyr; being part of his world, but not entirely part of it, he is always forced to being himself as he is—a man unwilling to wound the human dignity of a whore, able to accept the "necessary evils" of life with human grace, responsive to both the pain and value of human growth. He represents something far deeper and more complex than his fantasies of impotence; and in "Circe" he gets free of them at least

sufficiently for us to glimpse the irreducible unfathomable core of his being . . .

The catechism of "Ithaca" places him for our final, impersonal judgement . . . Reduced to his basic elements he still remains Everyman or Noman, the hidden Ulysses, "assumed by any or known to none." In this harsh light we perceive the dark center of life untouched, the spirit which has moved him all through.

Yeats's peasantry were receding even as he wrote his elegies for them and for their world as he imagined it to have been. Joyce, in Paris in 1920, studied maps of the Dublin of 1904, making certain that his details were accurate for that time and all in their proper place. Joyce was in exile, and in the more severe exile of time. Different as their political and literary stances were, both Joyce and Yeats were constructing and celebrating worlds that could be recaptured only within the mind; each thus gave his allegiance to the busy solitude and isolation of memory. Both wrote songs of survivors. Irony was the sign for Joyce of the strength of that mind; its distance from the materials that it manipulated. Just as for Yeats, elegy is the sign that the mind of the poet remains outside of any destruction it might imagine.

Yeats's technique for recapturing the lost world insures that the past remains lost. If it were to reappear the elegiac self would disappear into the poem. In the revolutionary moment, I asserted, poetic speech is the destruction and metamorphosis of the self, for to give meaning to the world is, at the same moment, to give shape to the self. In Yeats the revolutionary moment is seen through a haze of anxiety; the death of the self is seen as death itself. This must be avoided. In metaphysical systems of the absence of Presence, the absence of Being, what is being avoided is the time of continuous transformation that is the true life of the word. Anxiety about death causes us to make the absence (the death that is at the center of the continually creative self, which dies in every metaphor, which dies metaphorically) into an absolute absent presence, one that allows for a continuous, constant searching motion, but a self that remains as it is in that motion.

The symbol becomes not a presence but an absence. "The word is not the expression of a thing," Blanchot writes, "but rather the absence of this thing. The word makes the thing disappear, and imposes upon us the feeling of universal want." Marcuse writes: "The absent must be made present, because the greater part of the truth is in that which is absent." The absent must be made present, but it cannot be, except as a more profound absence, a negation. There is a similarity, Marcuse notes, between "negative dialectics" and the symbolist poet; both are ways of negation, showing forth what is more real than reality, but showing it forth as an absence. Marcuse quotes Mallarmé's classic formulation: "Je dis une fleur et hors de l'oubli où ma voix relégue aucun contour, en tant que quelque chose d'autre que les calices sus, musicalement se lève, idée même et suave, l'absente de tous bouquets." (I say a flower! and out of oblivion where my voice banishes all contours, musically rises, different from every known blossom, the one absent from all bouquets—Idea itself and delicate.)

These flowers cannot be touched; this absence cannot nourish. Yeats wrote:

Hic.
Dante Alighieri, so utterly found himself
That he has made that hollow face of his
More plain to the mind's eye than any face
But that of Christ.

Ille.
        And did he find himself
Or was the hunger that had made it hollow
A hunger for the apple on the bough
Most out of reach? . . . .

The gesture of the symbolist is locked off forever from this world, for it exists only in the self. It can be understood only by "divination"; that is, by a response that translates the auditor into the other world. If it enters this world it is as an absence, or, as in Yeats, in words of elegy. But this absence allows for constant motion by the poet. To construct a language as if it had a proper home, a moment when word matched with thing, self with world, and to make the attaining of this proper home a moment that is impossible within our world, our language, is to allow us to long continually for a moment of transformation that will never come, that cannot come, that must be forever longed for.

In Yeats's work we can see how absence allows the poet to construct a self that is in permanent mourning, longing for what is missed; and it is the very fact that something is always missed that guarantees the integrity of the self, and that the self-in-mourning may continue. Longing is a narcissistic desire for what can be found only as absent within the world, for what can be invoked only within the self. The self will never be transformed by this desire; a secure self is one constructed around a guarded absence, a permanent nostalgia.

Yet the death that we attempt to escape returns to haunt us. If we were to attain the world that we wish for, that we mourn for, it would be our death—not the metaphorical death that we were avoiding by this ruse of longing—but our literal death; absolute self-presence with the world would be to be locked indissolubly into it, unable to move. This union that we long for is, if we attain it, our death; its absence is a deferment of death, a suspended sentence. (The revolutionaries of "Easter, 1916" attain this union the only way that it can be attained: they die.)

Yeats himself tells a story that shows that the end of the longing that we have created to make a self is death and that life, under these conditions, is a striving for an atonement that fortunately we cannot attain. In "The Tables of the Law," Owen Aherne has a volume of secret teachings that will allow for his being to "return home to its former state," that will "gather [him] into eternity like doves into their dove-cots." But this teaching destroys him, not because of its falsity, but because of its truth. Yeats meets Aherne many years after Aherne has shown him the book of teachings, and Aherne is "a lifeless mask with dim eyes."

> "Has the philosophy of the *Liber inducens in Evanglium aeternum* made you very unhappy?" I said.
> "At first I was full of happiness," he replied, "for I felt a divine ecstasy, an immortal fire in every passion, in every hope, in every desire, in every dream; and I saw, in the shadows under leaves, in the hollow waters, in the eyes of men and women, its image, as in a mirror; and it was as though I was about to touch the Heart of God. Then all changed and I was full of misery; and in my misery it was

revealed to me that man can only come to that Heart through the sense of separation from it which we call sin, and I understood that I could not sin, because I had discovered the law of my being, and I understood that God has made a simple and an arbitrary law that we may sin and repent!"

. . . .

I went nearer to him and said, "Prayer and repentance will make you like other men."

"No, no," he said, "I am not among those for whom Christ died, and this is why I must be hidden. I have a leprosy that even eternity cannot cure. I have seen the whole, and how can I come again to believe that a part is the whole? I have lost my soul because I have looked out of the eyes of the angels."

Affirmations of the autonomous ego, no matter how constructed, were ones that Joyce, I think, became dubious about in the years that followed the writing of *Ulysses.* The novel was begun at the outbreak of World War I, the first war in which forces of mass propaganda through mass media were mobilized. World War I showed that the voices inside us and those outside could not be easily controlled. Neither parody nor the other distancing effect that Joyce used in *Ulysses* would be effective against the onslaught. Identity— Bloom's identity, our own—was a little more malleable than *Ulysses* finally admits. Even the irreducible core of a man like Bloom—supposing that there is such a thing—can be manipulated into telling lies, into wanting useless things, useless wars. We are easily persuaded to go off to slaughter each other, perhaps because, as Tolstoy says in the epilogue to *War and Peace,* we are not being "convinced" or "manipulated" by our leaders; rather we make our leaders up so that we will be allowed to indulge in our taste for killing others; we can say we were only following orders; we are released from the constraints of conscience. Bloom, or other members of his class, would collaborate in this slaughter. People would prefer the heroic to the sane and joyful mock-heroic, prefer repeating the voices to finding their own voice. It begins to appear that effective propaganda did not make one repeat an alien voice: it was our own voice all along; we sent the voice along a wire and it has returned to us.

Perhaps that is a way to read the incident of Bloom making

up a story of his time with Gerty, a story that she might read. He, the image of the artificer, hardly stands outside his creation. The artist conjectures about the response of his audience; the advertising man polls to find out what response his advertising campaign might receive. One method is more effective than the other, but the intent is not necessarily different. "Planned production" Marshall McLuhan writes, "means that the total process must be worked out in exact stages, backwards, like a detective story. In the first great age of mass production of commodities, and of literature as a commodity for the market, it became necessary to study the consumer's experience. In a word it became necessary to examine the effect of art and literature before producing anything at all."

Ironic distance too begins to seem questionable. Some people read popular fiction, some watch television, and some do these things in order to make up theories about them, to see what the masses are thinking. They read or watch ironically. But the ironic distance of the theorist more and more seems meaningless—just another way to read popular fiction, to watch television. The voices cannot be resisted through silence, exile, and cunning, or through the critical and withdrawn intellect.

Bloom, the advertising canvasser of 1904, is an early ideologue of the consumer society. "What is a home without Plumtree's Potted Meat? Incomplete," is a joke in *Ulysses*. But, as the surrealist noted, a joke repeated often enough, repeated over and over, becomes strangely threatening. The idea of incompleteness, of lack, is at the basis of the consumer society, and of neurosis. But we are always seeking something—always losing it, never attaining it securely—and around this busy seeking we construct our self.

Without a new Mustang you are incomplete, or new clothes, or . . . this lack, in a not very comical way, dominates our life. If we walk into eternity along Sandymount Strand the voice in our heads is less likely to be talking of Aristotle and the form of forms than of Dodge Swingers, 8 billion sold, fuel shortages, terrorist attacks, and the Real Thing—which is not the Logos but Coca-Cola. Aristotle begins to seem only another consumer item himself, though one that appeals to fewer people than Big Macs do.

It is not that a stronger therapy than *Ulysses* is needed to make us see what we are doing, who we are. Identity is the traces of other voices, those "traces of past identifications," that Freud said were the definition of character; our self is a collection of things bought by the ego to fill its lack. Where is our own voice, our own true and indivisible self, our one identity?

Nowhere.

CHATTERED

The appeals of advertising are made to an imaginary individuality. They are predicated at bottom on the fear that one lacks something, a void to be filled, which if only it were filled would make one complete, free from anxiety, self-sufficient, undying. Advertising proposes a fetishistic fixation on an object, the object that one can take into oneself by purchasing, to make one complete. But the absence confronts one everywhere; it can be repressed or denied, but the very denial indicates to the self that something is denied, speaks therefore of its opposite. Everything denied by the ego speaks, as the words of the elegy do, of what is missing, what is sought for, what cannot be found. And whatever is purchased becomes by being purchased unreal; it becomes one of the things of elegy, part of the lost world. Taking something inside (by purchase, by identification) makes it unreal. The more that is added (the more that is spoken of, that is *imaged*, that we attempt to duplicate or bring nearer by language, the more that is made unreal) the more that something more, something else, must be sought for.

The imaginary individuality of egoism is the denial of this vampiric sense of lack; and this false individuality keeps us from seeing our true similarity to each other, even while creating behind our backs a false one, as consumers. But to see this similarity, this communion, to accept the absence of personality—what Beckett called in speaking of *Finnegans Wake* "the absolute absence of the Absolute"—each would have to surrender his individuality, surrender his ghostly loved objects, those persons and things that we have taken into the ego as the poet of the elegy takes the lost world into his imagination, possessing it by losing it.

Finnegans Wake proposes a new answer to the question of

identity, and a new answer to the Cyclops—or a deeper acceptance of the classic answer. In *Ulysses* the self maintains itself in the language of lies; and there is something more—the black dot—than the lies can contain. The self is the single individual who when "reduced by cross multiplications of reverses of fortune . . . and by elimination of all positive values to a negligible irrational unreal quantity" is still someone somewhere rendering up his account, saying, in whatever manner he can, "Lord, here I am," to his author, the fabulous artificer. The self-contained self takes its form, its center, from a larger form-giving self, (the artist, the creator, the point of origin, the Absolute) that stands—Stephen asserts in *A Portrait*—outside his creation, paring his fingernails. Outside, perhaps, but present everywhere in the sense we are supposed to have of "completeness of form," the completeness that gives him the freedom to pare his nails. The identity and coherence of the creator is both sign and guarantee of the identity and final coherence of the character, and vice versa; the two figures point at each other. The origin guarantees that the self of the character is in its proper place, that it is complete in itself, self-understanding, self-created.

But the escape from history, from nationalism, from the pseudo-identities that society offers (and it is no longer clear that there is some other kind of identity) is to say to the question "Who are you?" that one is "No Man," nothing, nobody, the null set, who by being empty and without center, is everywhere, is everyone else.

Each of us, as we are seen in *Finnegans Wake*, is the creation of the others (even when one feels oneself to be in opposition, one is playing out a socially created role, that of rebel or scapegoat). And the other is himself not consciousness as it understands itself, is present to itself; he also is created by others. Each of us, one might say, is the creation of the other, his or her care, a joint-stock company in all meridians.

"Is there," Yeats asked rhetorically, "a nation-wide multi-form reverie, every mind passing through a stream of suggestion and the streams acting upon one another, no matter how distant the mind, how dumb the lips?" The question is answered affirmatively in the *Wake*; it is its working supposition. Yeats also answered yes, and the role this reverie implied for Yeats was that of seer, speaking for the dumb lips—dumb most especially because they were dead; the Great Mind, repository of symbols, was the thought of the dead. The yes of the *Wake* to this question is slightly different and would have required a humbling, a hollowing out of the Yeatsian personality, the Yeatsian self. Or if this humbling—as in "The Circus Animals' Desertion"—is done in relation to a pride or power still covertly believed in, affirmed even as it is put down, then what is required is not a humbling but a shattering (a chattering).

"NO IDEAS BUT IN THINGS"

In *Finnegans Wake* Joyce still takes on the role of seer. There are some steps that cannot be taken within art works, and one of them is the abolition of the audience. But Joyce does transform his role: he is not the Yeatsian high priest, but the "holy clown." Joyce's language, his stance, and technique change our conception of the nature of the subject matter of art, the means of artistic production, the nature of the creative act, and so call into question the status of the artist as one who creates out of nothing; who gives meaning; or who purifies.

For the *Wake* is made up of rubbish, of the broken bits of past history; which is to say pieces of language, old stories, chronicles, nursery rhymes, ballads, high talk, music hall lyrics, baby talk; even the trees and stones get in a word or two. "He that has eyes to see and ears to hear," Freud wrote, "may convince himself that no mortal man can keep a secret. If his lips are silent, he chatters with his finger-tips; betrayal oozes out of him at every pore. And thus the task of making conscious the most hidden recesses of the mind is one which it is quite possible to accomplish." The dumb lips were never dumb after all, but talking in different ways—continually, if only one had the ears to hear, the eyes to see. And Joyce's contribution was "merely" the arrangement of these fragments of speech. "I am quite content to go down to posterity as a scissors and paste man for that seems to me a harsh but not unjust description."

Joyce, in Lévi-Strauss's term, is a *bricoleur,* the jack-of-all-trades, the man who does not create his instruments, his tools, his materials, for a specific purpose but fits what he has lying around to the job at hand. The myth-maker, Lévi-Strauss writes, is a *bricoleur*, using bits of other myths, odds and ends of language, to make the new myth. Mythical thought "works by analogies and comparisons even though its creations, like those of the bricoleur, always consist of a new arrangement of elements, the nature of which is unaffected by whether they figure in the instrumental set or in the final arrangement (these being the same, apart from the internal disposition of their parts); 'it would seem that mythological worlds have been built up, only to be shattered again, and that new worlds were built from the fragments.'"

As opposed to the mythological bricoleur, Lévi-Strauss contrasts the "engineer" who "questions the universe . . . The engineer is always trying to make his way out and go beyond the constraints imposed by a particular state of civilization while the bricoleur by inclination or necessity always remains within them. This is another way of saying that the engineer works by means of concepts and the bricoleur by means of signs. One way . . . in which signs can be opposed to concepts is that whereas concepts aim to be wholly transparent with respect to reality, signs allow and even require the interposing and incorporation of a certain amount of human culture into reality." The engineer wants to transcend the particular state of civilization; he wishes his statement to be "transparent to reality." In Joyce's terms he wishes, as Stephen states in *Ulysses*, to "wake up" from the nightmare of history. The engineer wishes to see things clearly, without ideological mystification. But the author of the *Wake* has given up the project of waking up from history; rather, like Williams in *Paterson*, he plunges into it. The motion from *Ulysses* to *Finnegans Wake* is one from accepting a modest, nonrhetorical, chastened, sane, and healthy place—separate from the flux of events, the stream of propaganda, the junk of the world, its ideological debris—to one where history has become the very substance of one's being. One cannot here find a point outside history (the *Wake* closes on itself), but must find oneself within the materials. Or as Williams says, "no ideas but in things."

Jacques Derrida comments on bricoleur and engineer:

If one calls bricolage the necessity of borrowing one's concepts from the text of a heritage which is more or less coherent or ruined, it must be said that every discourse is *bricoleur*. The engineer . . . should be the one to construct the totality of his language, syntax and lexicon. In this sense the engineer is a myth. A subject who would supposedly be the absolute origin of his own discourse and would supposedly construct it "out of nothing," "out of whole cloth," would be the creator of the *verbe*, the *verbe* itself. The notion of the engineer who had supposedly broken with all forms of bricolage is therefore a theological idea; and since Lévi-Strauss tells us elsewhere that bricolage is mythopoetic, the odds are that the engineer is a myth produced by the *bricoleur*.

History is the materials for bricolage; its continuation is another creation of the jack-of-all-trades. There is no moment of origin to be appealed to or returned to, no moment when we confront the world and give it meaning, as Adam named the animals. (Perhaps Adam too only read the markings of God's script.) We are all perpetual beginners, in "a world made fresh," and there is nothing to be elegized. Our position is not more fallen than that of previous generations; each generation confronts a text to be interpreted.

There is no first text, beyond what one sees. This loss of authorship permeates the *Wake,* another face of the absolute absence of the Absolute. When loss is so permanent, elegy is impossible.

THE REVOLUTIONARY MOMENT

Joyce, who said about the *Wake,* "Really it is not I who am writing this book. It is you and you and you and that man over there, and that girl at the next table," accepted a radical chattering. He found himself lost right at home, diving inside to discover everyone already there, in the language. Stephen is again locked together with the old man, his demonic opponent, but it is no longer a struggle; if not an identity, it is at least an embrace. And as with any instance of love, Stephen must transform himself by giving himself up to the other. Joyce's work, despite (or perhaps including) the careful

structure of motifs, is near madness, a surrender of control. Joyce
is babbling, chattering. The enormous learning in each word, the
care, succeeds in this project by being too much learning; consciousness defeats itself and attains the power of the daimonic, of
unconsciousness, overdetermination. *Finnegans Wake*'s words are
overdetermined in the way the words of a dream are (or as words
chosen by chance might be); the sword of certainty never falls.
The almost pathologically neat marshaling of themes and motifs
can be seen as the work of a maker nearly overwhelmed by the
forces of language he has unleashed. That Joyce had been overwhelmed is the way Yeats read Joyce. Yeats "thought he perceived
in Joyce a destruction of the conscious mind's intelligible structure,
a loss of conscious control to the point almost of automatism."
Yeats wrote of Joyce: " . . . a philosophy like that of the Samskara
school of ancient India, mental and physical objects alike material,
a deluge of experience breaking over us and within us, melting
limits whether of line or thing; man no hard bright mirror dawdling
by the dry sticks of a hedge, but a swimmer, or rather the waves
themselves. In this new literature . . . man in himself is nothing."

Man in himself is nothing. Joyce opens himself to "you
and you and you and that man over there" as Baudelaire opened
himself to the crowd (though the differences also are instructive):

> The man who can easily wed the crowd knows a feverish enjoyment which
> will be eternally denied to the egoist, shut up like a trunk . . . What
> men call love is very meagre . . . compared to this ineffable orgy, to this
> holy prostitution of the soul that abandons itself entirely, poetry and
> charity included, to the unexpected arrival, the passing stranger. . . .
>
> The founders of colonies, the pastors of peoples, missionary
> priests exiled to the ends of the earth, doubtless know something of
> this mysterious drunkenness; and, in the heart of the vast family which
> their genius has created for itself, they must laugh sometimes at those
> who pity them for their destiny that is so unquiet and for their life that
> is so chaste.

And yet Joyce's words, Joyce's world, is not like that of the founder
of colonies or the missionary; it is not a peopling of one's solitude
by one's genius. The abandonment to the crowd in *Finnegans Wake*
reveals that the crowd is present in the language itself.

Finnegans Wake is a language in which we are each other's writing. (Lévi-Strauss found totemism to be the organization of a social discourse in which the women exchanged were the words.) One does not form others, as Baudelaire's poem implies; they create oneself, one's books; they speak you. It is by allowing this creation to happen that the crowd, the language appears:

> While he could "do anything with language" he believed that some-how the spirit of language was working through him of its own volition. An anecdote given by Richard Ellmann shows Joyce's unusual attitude: "Beckett was taking dictation from Joyce for *Finnegans Wake*; there was a knock on the door and Joyce said, 'Come in.' Beckett who hadn't heard the knock by mistake wrote down 'Come in' as part of the dictated text. Afterwards he read it back to Joyce who said, "What's that 'Come in'?" "That's what you dictated," Beckett replied. Joyce thought for a moment realizing that Beckett hadn't heard the knock; then he said. "Let it stand." The very fact that the misunderstanding occurred in actuality gave it prestige for Joyce. This incident shows . . . Joyce was not in his own opinion simply writing a book, he was performing a work of magic.

We say, speaking of psychoanalytic ideas of projection, that the subjectivity of characters creates new characters: phantoms (or so we think). But projection happens always. The permeability of personalities is so high that it is difficult to talk of intersubjectivity, as if there were separate subjectivities, as if there were more than one subject or less than a constantly circulating mob of them. As with individuality, we confront in the idea of intersubjectivity that hollow in us, that space that others invade, occupy, colonize with meaning, leave their messages in; as if we were wombs, surrounding the other. By becoming a womb the lack is turned into a substance. But the lack in *Finnegans Wake* has no outer substance. Each person is a text to the other; the scribbling takes place not in, but on other scribbling. The image used is of a palimpsest, but the palimpsest itself is made out of words. Character, in *Finnegans Wake,* is not an "identity" with oneself; it is transpersonal, not central—like the black dot—but total, and thus unnameable by any particular word within language. (Like the medieval definitions of God, its center is everywhere, its circumference nowhere.) Insofar as characters have identities in this novel they come not from things being in their proper places (where self matches up with description of self in that endless description we offer ourselves to be sure that everything is in its place, that nothing is missing) but from puns, from words straying from their proper sense. Meaning in this book comes from language straying out of its place, from worlds colliding. Identity does not belong to oneself but is created by others, by writing straying into and onto other writing. The *Wake* allows words to "get on top of each other and become sexual" allowing a third word (third world) to be born, a Character in its own right, with its own part to play, the part of disappearing into another pun.

The search for the proper sense of words (before they strayed from sense and began punning, a sense where words match up with things and the world makes sense) is a search in high good spirits that keeps *Finnegans Wake* circling. There is always a secret (what HCE did in the park; or the letter the hen has hidden or scratched up in the rubbish heap—is it a letter or litter?). The secret will make sense of things, bring the dream to an end, allow us to wake up perhaps from this nightmare of history. But each pun in this case is an illustration that we don't make our history as we wish; to make sense at all, to move forward is not to make sense exactly, but to say more, or something other, than one means. A pun turns language, turns sense, back upon itself.

Poetry here is a slip away from the "proper sense". There is symbolism from the beginning; our first sense impressions are imaginative, poetic ones; our bodies themselves are poetic creations, misinterpretations of how the world works, in a world that only has misinterpretations. The *Wake* accepts our inability to get things right, our inability to bring the play to an end, accepts "the absolute absence of the Absolute," turning the search into farce.

There is here nothing which isn't poetry, a slip away from sense. There is no alienated spirit behind or beyond appearances, whose step on the stage will bring the play to an end. The unconscious in the *Wake* is an open secret, expressed always in jokes, slips of the pen, puns, slips of the tongue, Freudian slips, poetry; and the only sense we have is a slippery poetic one. The next meaning is not a true sense, but a different interpretation, following a different line to a different conclusion that is a new beginning. The bricoleur only re-arranges, re-reads what is already there; he creates "a new arrangement of elements, the nature of which is unaffected by whether they figure in the instrumental set or in the final arrangement (these being the same, apart from the internal disposition of their parts)." There is a formulation of Yeats's that reveals what the true nature of "the alienated spirit,"—the absolute that would put an end to the poem—is. "According to Rilke a man's death is born with him," Yeats wrote, "and if his life is successful and he escapes mere 'mass death,' his nature is completed by a final union with it." Death is the thing not expressed within the materials; to see through the world is to be joined with one's death. "All images can be dissolved only after the most painful and rigorous self-examination," Ellmann writes of Yeats's theory, "this moment of completeness of perfection, of Unity of Being, is the moment of death." For Yeats there is something more, something behind and beneath sensuous experience; the world can be seen through, and if seen through utterly, the body dies. In *Finnegans Wake* the transcendent realm is always present here and now: there is another world, but it is this one. Death is not deferred, but is present always and in each moment. To accept the death in each moment is to hear the silence within words.

Silence and speech reconciled, or death present in each moment, or absence and presence at once: for Derrida the "myth of presence" of a world fully present to us, the exact expression our consciousness, transparent, is the myth of the precedence of speech over writing, the meaning present to us as the voice is present within the throat. Writing—which Derrida says preceded speech—is predicated on a difference between consciousness and the thing symbolized, between sign and thing, between sign and sign; there is an absence always; the word signifies what is not present. But there is a rabbinical story that both the written law and the oral commentary were given to Moses on Mount Sinai at the same moment. *Finnegans Wake* has what we might imagine to be a main text, a written text (the "plain ten commandments" as Bloom calls them) —the words as orthography, as the letters on the page suggest them

—and a commentary, the sound of the words, the second meanings, suggested by the sounds, the puns, the sur-text. But they are both there at once. One is always turning into the other. The sur-text becomes by some turn the main text for a time, then dives back under. The unconscious is always present; it is never really present nor ever absent. It is always peek-a-booing, so we don't know which is which or where we are. "But by writing thithaways end to end and turning, turning and end to end thithaways writing and with lines of litters slittering up and louds of latters slettering down, the old semetomyplace and jupetbackagain from tham Let Rise till Hum Lit. Sleep, where in the waste is the wisdom?

"Letting pun play pass to ernest," it says in *Finnegans Wake*, reminding one of *The Importance of Being Earnest*. Wilde's play jokes, as *Ulysses* does, on the nature of the real, the proper name for a person. Bloom, too, like Ernest and Jack goes "bunburying," looking for a lover under an assumed name. But in Wilde's play the action ends when the pun is completed, and the play moves toward the transformation of the name. Our names are masks, used to pursue our ends, or perhaps one should say the way our ends pursue themselves. And the lover too wears a mask. Wilde ends with the discovery that we all wear masks.

Finnegans Wake accepts this conclusion as its perpetual beginning. It never stops bunburying. It lets pun play pass to ernest. The end point in the Wilde play is the starting point of the *Wake*, not an assumption to be demonstrated, but taken for granted. The Wilde play presents a series of masks; the *Wake* a series of metamorphoses. The making of a metaphor, or a pun, does not here illuminate the first term of the metaphor but rather turns the first term into the second, as egg whites are turned or folded into chocolate. The thing named becomes the self—an interpenetration both ways; the line of the dramatic action shifts around this new self, following perhaps the echo or overtone of some pun off into its frame of reference (which was always a part of this frame).

The word *mask* implies a person behind the mask and to say that usually personality is fiction implies that there is something of personality that might be nonfiction. But in *Finnegans Wake* there is only mistaken identity; what is being represented is itself only another metaphor. There is no master of the language in the *Wake*, no one who creates the person who is being represented as if from whole cloth. The chorus being represented is the language itself in its permutations and metamorphoses and it cannot be named. (It is not named, but it is visible in the motion from metaphor to metaphor; not a noun but an unnameable verb.) What we call character in the *Wake* is the makings of language, not vice versa; it is dispersed throughout the words, not using them but being shown forth by them; character becomes anagrams, as we are to know the presence of HCE by the appearance, from time to time, of his initials "littered" throughout the text.

The language of the *Wake* is not mimetic. The language of mimesis assumes a separation between words and things and a self that uses the language. About *Finnegans Wake* Samuel Beckett said, "It is not about something. It is that something itself." Nothing is named here, held on to by language, duplicated, restored, fixed. The language is rather the language by which a world is created, which is to say, by which a self is created. The language which does not name but creates a self cannot be "used." The speaker cannot know beforehand the meanings of his words, for his words make him. The man is necessarily speaking at each moment, or being spoken by (the motions are here indistinguishable) an unknown tongue. *Finnegans Wake* is glossolalia. Tropes become momentary deities that give a new shape to the interpreter who speaks the tropes in new words. This, I think, is the language, the revolutionary moment that Mandlestam speaks of in his essay "The Word and Culture":

> A heroic era has begun in the life of the word. The word is flesh and bread. It shares the fate of flesh and bread: suffering . . . People are hungry . . . These days something like glossolalia manifests itself. In a sacred frenzy, poets speak in the language of all times, all cultures. Nothing is impossible. Just as a room where a man is dying is opened to all, so the door of the old world is flung wide before the crowd. Suddenly everything has become common property. Come in and help yourself. Everything's available: all the labyrinths, all the hiding places, all the forbidden paths. The word has become, not a seven-stop, but a thousand-stop reed, instantly animated by the breathing of all ages. In glossolalia the most striking thing is that the speaker does not know the language in which he speaks. He speaks in a totally unknown tongue.

HISTORY
AS
THEATER;
OR, TERROR
AND
SACRIFICE

HAMLET

One is told that the Russians now disapprove of tragedy, and that there was a performance of *Hamlet* in the Turk-Sib region which the audience decided spontaneously was a farce. They may well hold out against the melancholy of old Russia, and for them there may be dangerous implications in tragedy which other people do not see.
—EMPSON, *Some Versions of Pastoral*

I wonder, in thinking about this story of Empson's, and in thinking about *Hamlet,* what the dangerous implications of tragedy are? I wonder what changes in the conditions of our lives and in how we think about them would be necessary for us to see *Hamlet* as farce? The time before the revolution was, Marx said, the prehistory of mankind. After the revolution the free determination of humanity would begin—their real history, made by those who are fully conscious. In the terms of *Hamlet,* one might say that people had moved beyond the world of seeming, of appearances; they no longer need to be deceived or deceive themselves about the real conditions of their lives; they would be objective. They would see things as they are. For Marx, to hope for an end to history as we have known it was to hope for an end to tragedy, or rather to the tragedy of history. It is the same thing, I think, to hope as Joyce's Dedalus did that he might wake up from the "nightmare of history." When we wake up the nightmare is revealed as having been a nightmare, and the tragedy of history—which is the tragedy of *Hamlet*—becomes a farce to us. (If, that is, we can escape from the melancholy of Old Russia.)

Both history and tragedy are sad stories of the death of

61

kings. Shakespeare's *Romeo and Juliet* is one of the few tragedies up to that time which, though still about aristocrats, is not about persons highly placed in the state—persons, in fact, upon whom the fate of the state rests. In all of Shakespeare's other tragedies the fate of the nation is implicated in the fate of the main characters.

> The cess of majesty
> Dies not alone, but like a gulf, doth draw
> What's near with it; or it is a massy wheel
> Fixed on the summit of the highest mount,
> To whose huge spokes ten thousand lesser things
> Are mortised and adjoined, which when it falls,
> Each small annexment, pettty consequence,
> Attends the boisterous ruin. Never alone
> Did the King sigh, but with a general groan.   [3.311–23]

In fact, the fate of the cosmos generally seems to the king's subjects to hang on the monarch's fate. Horatio says:

> In the most high and palmy state of Rome,
> A little ere the mightiest Julius fell
> The graves stood tenantless and the sheeted dead
> Did squeek and gibber in the Roman streets;
> As stars with trains of fire and dews of blood,
> Disasters in the sun; and the moist star,
> Upon whose influence Neptune's empire stands,
> Was sick almost to doomsday with eclipse.
> And even like the precurse of feared events
> As harbingers preceeding still the fates
> And prologue to the omen coming on,
> Have heaven and earth together demonstrated
> Unto our climature and countrymen.   [1.1.112–25]

When the king falls, all fall. Or perhaps it is better to say that the people, the subjects, choose to think it so, to have it so. They are very interested spectators to the fate of kings; his story is in some sense their story, and not only because his decrees will affect their livelihoods. For tragedy grew out of sacred rites, where the chorus articulated for itself a representative: a priest, god, king. His death then was part of the ritual, a sacrifice offered by all of them, an atonement, a blood payment for all. If this is so then it is in fact true, as Hamlet says jokingly, that "our outstretched heroes" are "the beggars' shadows."

For a nation to enter on the stage of history (and history, as *Hamlet* repeatedly reminds us, is a stage), it must articulate for itself a representative, a hero, a leader, a king. Like the leader of the chorus, the king is the people's actor. History is the record of the fate of kings, of the wars by which representatives try to put down other representatives.

We are told such a story at the beginning of *Hamlet:*

>   our last king
> Whose image even but now appeared to us,
> Was, as you know, by Fortinbras of Norway,
> Thereto pricked on by a most emulate pride,
> Dared to the combat; in which our valiant Hamlet
> (For so this side of our known world esteemed him)
> Did slay this Fortinbras, who by a sealed compact
> Well ratified by law and heraldry,
> Did forfeit, with his life, all those his lands
> Which he stood seized of, to the conqueror.
> . . . .
>   Now, sir, young Fortinbras,
> Of unimproved mettle hot and full,
> Hath in the skirts of Norway here and there
> Sharked up a list of lawless resolutes,
> For food and diet, to some enterprise
> That hath a stomach in't; which is no other,
> As it doth well appear unto our state,
> But to recover of us by strong hand
> And terms compulsatory, those foresaid lands
> So by his father lost; . . .   [1.1.80–104]

As the king is our actor, we are his audience. (We made him up, perhaps, and then forgot we did so.) We are audience to his tragedy and participate in it vicariously, and perhaps his fall remains, as in the sacred rite, our atonement, our offering. In any case, for the king, all the world is a stage. So waking up, bringing history to an end, and bringing tragedy to an end (historical tragedy) may be similar jobs.

History, in Shakespeare's plays, is a bloody business. When

viewed from the outside (as if there were an outside) it looks almost meaningless, without goal or purpose. Jan Kott writes:

> Each of these great historical tragedies begins with a struggle for the throne, or for its consolidation. Each ends with the monarch's death and a new coronation. In each of the Histories the legitimate ruler drags behind him a long chain of crimes. He has rejected the feudal lords who helped him to reach the crown; he murders first his enemies, then his former allies, he executes possible successors and pretenders to the crown. But he has not been able to execute them all. . . . a young prince returns—the son, grandson, or brother of those murdered—to defend the violated law . . . he personifies the hope for a new order and justice. But every step to power continues to be marked by murder, violence, treachery. And so, when the new prince finds himself near the throne, he drags behind him a chain of crimes as long as the legitimate ruler. When he assumes the crown he will be just as hated as his predecessor. He has killed enemies, now he will kill former allies. And a new pretender appears in the name of violated justice. The wheel has turned full circle . . .
>
> . . . .
>
> Emanating from the features of individual kings and usurpers in Shakespeare's History plays there gradually emerges the image of history itself. The image of the Grand Mechanism.

Murder, violence, treachery—a mechanism without meaning. There are similar descriptions in *War and Peace*. "In 1789 a ferment arises in Paris; it grows, spreads, and is expressed by a movement of peoples from west to east. Several times it moves eastward and collides with a counter-movement from the east westward. . . . During that twenty year period an immense number of fields were left untilled, houses were burned, trade changed its direction, millions of men migrated, were impoverished, or were enriched and millions of Christian men professing the law of love of their fellows slew one another."

Or this is history as it is expressed in two words in *Finnegans Wake,* "Killykill-killy." Or at the end of *Hamlet:*

> So shall you hear
> Of carnal bloody, and unnatural acts,
> Of accidental judgements, casual slaughters,

Of deaths put on by cunning and forced cause
And, in this upshot, purposes mistook
Fall'n on the inventors' heads.   [5.5.381–86]

This is history without words, without the motives people give for
their actions; history as a dumbshow, like the prologue to the play
the court watches in *Hamlet*. History without words, without motives: in fact we are nowadays inclined to think that the motives the
actors gave were not the real ones. We substitute other motives. But,
some later age will show that the motives we substituted were not
the real ones but were only rationalizations offered by our age, or
some group in our age, that, having some project of its own, tried to
rewrite history for its own justification.

The Grand Mechanism, or history without motives, is the
struggle for power: whoever is near the throne will try to seize it.
And the corollary: history is written by the victors, by those who
succeed in seizing it. Thus whoever wins the throne expects for a
time to be justified in having it—justified by God and the people, but
in fact justified by the scribes who write history. In *Hamlet*, no one
of the main characters survives to write the play. Hamlet's justification remains ambiguous. We don't hear the story Horatio tells.

In any case, as long as there is a throne to be contested the
killing goes on. The king who lives out his reign, like Henry V, does
so, Shakespeare shows us, not because he is the Lord's anointed,
uniting a claim of legitimate succession with just rule, but because
he is clever. He unites the people behind an external war, selling the
venture with clever propaganda. (Part of this propaganda is that he
unites a just claim to the throne with a just rule.)

The mechanism described by Kott, and perhaps by Shakespeare, sounds a great deal like Nietzsche's will to power. There is
a character in *Hamlet* for whom the will to power, activity itself, is
sufficient; Fortinbras, whose name means strong-armed, seeks no
other justification for himself. Like old Hamlet, whose warlike
appearance is repeatedly stressed, he is a warrior, or perhaps he only
seems, for the moment, merely a warrior. Fortinbras will ascend to
the throne. This is not yet his play. He will need his justifications,
counselors; he will need reason, ideology, lies.

Superimposed on the world of history, on the will to power, history as dumb show, history without the words of the actors, superimposed, and seemingly in conflict with it, is the desire for a moral order, for justice. There is, as Kott says, an incompatibility between the moral order and history. He is speaking here of Richard II:

> the king lets slip a sentence that foreshadows the problems of Hamlet. And indeed Hamlet must only be interpreted in the light of the two Richard plays. This sentence expresses a sudden fear of the world and its cruel mechanism, from which there is no escape, but which one cannot accept. For there are not bad kings, or good kings; kings are only kings. Or let us put it in modern terms; there is only the king's situation and the system. This situation leaves no room for freedom of choice. At the end of the tragedy the King speaks a sentence that might be spoken by Hamlet:
> "They love not poison that do poison need . . ."
> In Shakespeare's world there is a contradiction between the order of action and the moral order. This contradiction is human fate. One cannot get away from it.

But perhaps this makes our problem too simple—I think it accepts the terms in which Hamlet at first would like to see his problem. For perhaps it is our desire for justification, for salvation, for a moral order, that keeps the mechanism of history going, that puffs the business on. The hero's death fulfilled a part of the ritual, a sacrifice offered, an atonement, a blood payment. History—kingship—is what gives us salvation. And because we need salvation we must have kings.

Hamlet wishes to revenge his father and so be atoned with him. He says the time is out of joint. But if we look at history as a dumbshow, the time is always out of joint. Hamlet, like the Communist Party, believes that he is come to set the time right. (When he kills Polonius, he thinks of himself as God's scourge and minister, although it is hard for me to see what purpose of heaven is served by Polonius's death. Or, for that matter, the deaths of Rosencrantz and Guildenstern who, trying to make their way, were innocent apparently of their mission.)

Perhaps not every moment is, as Marxists say, objectively revolutionary, but still the time is, for those who would see it that way, always out of joint. Historical activity then must be ceaseless, and the work of putting things right must go on continually.

"The time is out of joint," Hamlet says, "O cursed spite that ever I was born to set it right." O cursed spite—but there is no indication that he would have been happy simply to be Claudius's subject. Discontented from the first, he wished to be king. He says this only once, but it is the more telling for being so long absent from his list of grievances, and so obvious a one—that is, that Claudius "popped in twixt him and the election." He mentions once also that he is ambitious, and that as things stand now his ambition lacks scope. But this is not to say, I think, that Hamlet is duplicitous, rather that both motives, revenge and atonement with the father, and the desire to be king, are hand in hand. They are the story of kingship, of the family and the state.

The time is always out of joint, someone has always murdered the king. (Old Hamlet, remember, has killed old Fortinbras. In fair armed combat perhaps, but young Fortinbras does not see it that way. He wants his uncle's land back, wants revenge, wants perhaps to be atoned with "the father" and to replace him.)

The king's murder must be atoned, must be avenged; but a father has always just died:

> ... Fie tis a fault to Heaven,
> A fault against the dead, a fault to nature,
> To reason most absurd, whose common theme
> Is death of fathers, and who still has cried
> From the first corse till he that died today,
> This must be so.   [1.2.101–5]

Claudius is the new father, the new king, and so would like to think that reason has always cried so. But this is not the case. We want our father's death and we feel guilty when it happens. There must be a sacrifice for it, there must be revenge. From that time till now all have cried like Hamlet: this cannot be.

Hamlet, like all those who wish to revenge their father's death, is a pale criminal. He is implicated in the crime he wants to punish, and so must, by his own logic, be punished also. (Fortinbras has a certain good fortune in this regard. His father lost something, and Fortinbras, in revenging him, not only replaces him, but restores him also.) Hamlet must want his own guilt—continually hinted at, never specified—to be uncovered also: "I am very proud, revengeful, ambitious, with more offenses at my beck than I have thoughts to put them in, imagination to give them shape, or time to act them in. What should such fellows as I do crawling between earth and heaven?" (3.1.124–29). Hamlet wants to die, and so must continue the play, prolong it, until he has the opportunity to kill Claudius and himself at once.

History, as a dumb show, is a bloody field, a stage littered with corpses. But the actors kill perhaps to justify themselves for the crime that they (we) have committed. We are guilty to want the throne, and guilty in having it; so either way there must be sacrifice, either of ourselves, or others, or—for the crime we are revenging is the one all wished to commit—all must die. For there to be blame and expiation there must be witnesses, moral witness, theater. (The world is a stage for all of us now, because everyman is a king.) Or the court is a stage on which a ritual of sacrifice and atonement is acted, a play in which we all vicariously participate.

Hamlet is about a court where a play takes place. But a court is already a stage, and courtiers are, as Harry Levin points out, not very different from actors. *Hamlet* has a play within a play within a play. But Prince Hamlet is uncomfortable with theater, he is uncomfortable with being an actor—and this in all senses of the word. He is uncomfortable with court life, with theatrical life, but this is the same as saying that he is fascinated by it. He cannot make it come out right, though he tries over and over in a variety of ways. He can neither accept having a role, a part to play, nor can he reject it.

In an early scene, Hamlet says:

Seems Madam? Nay, it is. I know not "seems".
Tis not alone my inky cloak, good mother,
Nor customary suits of solemn black,
Nor windy suspiration of forced breath,
No, nor the fruitful river in the eye,
Nor the defected havior of the visage
Together with all forms, moods, shapes of grief,

That can denote me truly. These indeed seem.
For they are actions that a man might play,
But I have that within me which passes show;
These but the trappings and suits of woe.   [1.2.76-86]

But, in fact, he does know seeming. He pretends to be mad,
pretends he's mad from love of Ophelia, and at the play's end he
tries lying to Laertes to clear himself of Polonius's murder:

This presence knows, and you must need have heard,
How I am punished with a sore distraction.
What I have done
That might your nature, honor, and exception
Roughly awake, I here proclaim was madness.
Was't Hamlet wronged Laertes? Never Hamlet.
If Hamlet from himself be ta'en away,
And when he's not himself does wrong Laertes,
Then Hamlet does it not, Hamlet denies it.   [5.2.229-37]

Hamlet offers his feigned madness as an excuse for a real killing.

Hamlet knows how to act, he wants to be king, to have
an audience, to act a part. To be a king is to act a part for others,
in every sense. The King was once the Lord's anointed, and the
play he enacted part of a sacred ritual for us, his subjects, his audience.
But now, though the play continues, there is, as Claudius knows,
as Hamlet knows, no divine providence in kingship. Claudius says:

Do not fear our person.
There's such divinity doth hedge a king
That reason can but peep to what it would,
Act little of his will.   [4.5.123-25]

But both Hamlet and Claudius know this to be a lie—for he has
killed a king. It is, like his speech to Hamlet, a way to convince
Laertes that treason is impossible. This speech of providence in the
mouth of a regicide is revealed as ideology, as public relations.
A king is now a self-conscious actor for others, though the show
still goes on.

The part of Hamlet hardly makes sense unless Hamlet
thinks of himself as playing to an unseen audience. He speaks solil-
oquies, makes asides, reveals to us that he understands something
his auditors do not comprehend. He both wants and does not want

to have an audience, for to have an audience is to be a king, to replace his father. Thus his grief must be beyond show, inward. (For to show is to act, to make public, to "put on a show"—to make a show is to be a little separate from one's grief, a manipulator of it, somehow insincere.

Is it show, or is it real? Hamlet worries this question continually, forcing Polonius and Osric to lie, to prove they are courtiers, and thus necessarily liars.

> Hamlet. Do you see yonder cloud that's almost in shape of a camel?
> Polonius. By the 'mass and 'tis like a camel indeed.
> Hamlet. Methinks it is like a weasel.
> Polonius. It is backed like a weasel.
> Hamlet. Or like a whale.
> Polonius. Very like a whale.   [3.2.384–90]

And again, as if he can't tire of the joke,

> Hamlet. I will receive it, sir, with all diligence of spirit. Put your
>   bonnet to his right use. 'Tis for the head
> Osric.   I thank your lordship it is very hot.
> Hamlet. No, believe me, 'tis very cold; the wind is northerly.
> Osric.   It is indifferent cold, my lord indeed.
> Hamlet. But yet methinks it is very sultry and hot for my complexion.
> Osric.   Exceedingly my lord; it is very sultry, as 'twere—I cannot
>   tell how.   [5.2.93–102]

He shows his obsession when he copies down a very obvious point: "one may smile and smile, and be a villain." He worries the question when he is worrying about death, for in death all appearances come to an end, as in Wallace Stevens's poem about the funeral: "Let be be finale of seem."

The whole court apparently knows that they are actors, but actors in a ritual gone awry, a ritual without divine providence, a ritual in which they are only "seeming," playing at their parts, or so they think, self-conscious actors. And so they are obsessed, like Hamlet, with finding out what is behind appearances. Polonius has a number of different stratagems for finding out the truth, like his clever way of discovering the bits about Laertes in Paris, or hiding in the Queen's chamber. Polonius is the secret police of Denmark.

Things are not what they seem. And yet, there is no life outside of this life; there is no life outside of history; no life outside of what we show each other. Things are not what they seem, and they *are* only what they seem: their reputation, the name that lives after them, what people call them. We have no language to escape this bind but that of tautology, (madness, madness, Polonius says) and madness—or madness with a method, which is poetry.

If things are not what they seem, and yet are not what we see, and yet are only what someone sees, then there *must* be, as Laertes demands, a God who sees. Or as Claudius says:

> In the corrupted currents of this world
> Offenses gilded hand may shove by justice,
> And oft tis seen the wicked prize itself
> Buys out the law. But tis not so above.
> There is no shuffling; there the action lies
> In his true nature, and we ourselves compelled
> Even to the teeth and forehead of our faults,
> To give in evidence.   [3.3.57-64]

I asked myself certain questions at the beginning of this essay that I now see I won't—oddly enough—be able to answer: How to bring history to an end? How to bring an end to tragedy?

Perhaps we think, like Hamlet, that we are actors and there-fore liars, but in fact we cannot lie. "So full of artless jealousy is guilt," Gertrude says, "It spills itself in fearing to be spilt." Or Lenin: "In order to know what the social democrats are thinking watch their hands, not their mouths." Or Freud: "He that has eyes to see and ears to hear may convince himself that no mortal man can keep a secret. If his lips are silent, he chatters with his finger-tips; betrayal oozes out of him at every pore." We can't lie; what we seem is what we are, although it is not what we think we are. Our presentation of ourselves might be artful or poetic, but it would be pointless to make it clever.

Or perhaps it is still a play but one which there are no privi-leged parts. The King acted for all of us in a drama where we were the audience. Enough of that. I don't mean that every man should become a king, but that we should bring the house down, burn up the theater. It is a symbolic drama, but the symbols are everywhere always. As Hamlet says, "There is a special providence in the fall of a sparrow." In any case no one is singled out to be God's minister, God's scourge.

Perhaps. But at the end of *Hamlet* the play goes on pretty much as usual. At his death Hamlet calls the others mutes and audience to his act—for now he can be King, can be an actor, for he is dying. He expiates assuming the throne as he does it. And he realigns the ritual. By dying he ceases to play at his part, but becomes it. Or almost: the time being as it is, it is necessary that someone tell his story, tell it properly, in an authorized version.

His body is conveyed to the stage.

In any case, the tragedy of history still goes on. The Turk-Sib peasants soon had a new little father in Stalin, who replaced their little father, the czar. The theater was open again every night, as usual, and the melancholy of old Russia returned.

PATTI HEARST

History had been "unleashed." . . . *The Bacchae* is the tragedy of the madness of Greece, the madness of rulers and of people. "You are mad, grievously mad, beyond the power of any drugs to cure, for you are drugged with madness.". . . In periods of madness, mad gods and their even madder prophets always appear. At the time of the Peloponnesian War new dark gods came from the east, south and north, demanding . . . bloody sacrifices: Attis, Sabazius, and Adonis, Bendis, Cybele and the Egyptian Iris with cow's horns.

—JAN KOTT, *The Eating of the Gods*

In 1972 and early '73 a young man, Herbert Mullins, killed thirteen people. Some were hitch-hikers; one was an old man (Mullins got telepathic messages from his parents telling him to kill the old man); one was a young woman whom he dissected (killed because of a "message" from a local naturalist); one was a priest; several were campers; the last was a man whom he shot while the man worked in his backyard. Mullins had spent time in a mental hospital, but when his condition responded to thorazine, he had been released. After his capture he was returned to the hospital for examination.

When Dr. Lunde assured him that he could halt the water bucket treatment, Mullins gradually opened up . . .

He announced that he had been chosen to promulgate the Philosophy of Jonah; to act out the theory that minor disasters prevent major disasters like earthquakes, floods, tornadoes and hurricanes. His special job was to prevent California from falling into the ocean because of a cataclysmic earthquake.

. . . . Herb said that he considered himself the "typical scapegoat" chosen to accept blame for the weaknesses of the rest of society.

73

"See people like to sing the die song. If I am a president of my class when I graduate from high school, I can tell two maybe possibly three young male homo sapiens to die. I can sing that song to them and they'll have to kill themselves or be killed. An automobile accident, a knifing, a gunshot wound."

These sacrifices would prove to God that the rest of humanity was interested enough so he would prevent earthquakes . . .

"They know this minor natural disaster averts a major natural disaster. Well, they let a guy go kill-crazy, a little homo-sapien bull, you know; he'd go kill-crazy, maybe twenty or thirty people . . . And they don't do anything. All they do is sing the die song, you know, 'go kill something for me.' They don't kill for themselves, the people that make the laws. They just protect themselves from a kill-crazy person.

"You take the seismograph, the number of earthquakes, their potency . . . the history of the wars, and you come out with a percentage of people that have been steadily dying in order to prove to the great Creator who created the earth and put it in orbit . . . just to prove to him that we are willing to die to keep the earth in orbit and the continents intact.

"You know, homo sapiens have found murder decreases the number of natural disasters and the extent of devastation. Therefore we will always have murder."

A THEATER OF SACRIFICE

The late Sixties seemed to me—as they did, of course, to many people—a hopeful time. It was thought to be a time of breakdown for our society, a breakdown that promised a new birth. It was a time of "greening"—the grass pushing up through the cracks in the sidewalk.

It was a time of dissolution (of social roles, of the mechanisms of control, of the sources of authority, of law and order, of the false relations between men and women, blacks and whites). Hope and breakdown were—it seemed—the same—"confusion/Basis of renewals," as Pound had written in an early Canto. One epoch was ending, and another, a far better one, was surely being born. It was the end of the Age of Aquarius, the final crisis of capitalism, a time of liberation (a word whose meaning seemed clear).

A time of "greening" then is also a time of breakdown; the city destroyed as the grass pushes up and over it; a time of earthquakes, the pushing upward from below. It is "the absolute liquefaction of every stable support," as Kojève says of the fear of death the slave feels in Hegel's *Phenomenology*. "By this fear . . . the slavish consciousness melted internally; it shuddered deeply and everything fixed or stable trembled within it." This is a time of great anxiety for those whose world is dying, coming to an end—and that, I think, is all of us. For the ego, like the unconscious, is collective; the death of our society, of the social ego, is the dissolution and "death" of every individual also.

Those who are losing control, those who feel anxiety, institute "terror"—a repression intended to stop the change, stop dissolution, keep the world as it is. Though this terror process may take a somewhat different shape in the case of radical terrorism and ruling class terror, it is, at bottom, the same process, and it is meant to bring about the same end—to stop the earthquake, to keep from "dying," to keep California from falling into the ocean.

The ruling class terrorizes those they rule to stop their (our) world from shaking apart, to freeze the rebellious, to halt their actions, to turn them to stone. By 1971 this terror had brought the hopeful period to an end. There had occurred in this country what Herbert Marcuse rather dramatically (perhaps melodramatically) described as "a pre-emptive counter-revolution." National guardsmen in Ohio fired into crowds of demonstrators; black students in Jackson, Mississippi were shot to death by state troopers; a Black Panther, Fred Hampton, was gunned down by government agents in Chicago. Policemen broke heads, and once or twice blinded demonstrators with gas or buckshot. This was a mild sort of terror by the standards of most countries—only a few were killed; not many at all; only a very few.

But it need not be many. It is entirely compatible with the terror process that only a few be killed. As E. V. Walter points out in *Terror and Resistance*, terror is a "theatrical procedure" requiring only a few actors and pointless without an audience to enjoy the drama. "Stripped to its essentials a dramaturgic model of the terror process would include three actors: a source of violence, a victim, and a target. The victim perishes, but the target reacts to the spectacle . . . with some manner of submission."

In the terror process one among many is chosen and killed

before the others. Terror fascinates the others, making them an audience and destroying their previous solidarity, and even as it isolates and atomizes them, replacing that solidarity with another one—a negative image of the first, a solidarity of fear. They are separate because insofar as they are like each other they are in danger. They must repress their similarity. Every man, insofar as I can be seen to be like him, is a threat to me, evidence against me (and yet we are alike). I project onto others those very qualities of similarity that are in myself and that are now dangerous to me. And in a new way we are absolutely the same; we are all afraid of the same external power. Terror turns the audience into units that are absolutely separate and absolutely the same: the stuff of modern government.

Our country at war had dealt in terror in Vietnam; there should have been no surprise when its pale form appeared here. (One of the slogans of young radicals as they threw rocks through store windows at demonstrations—"trashing" the stores—had been "Bring the War Home.") The war was terror: massive bombings, search and destroy missions, defoliation, automated battlefields, forced urbanization, pacification, the familiar litany of horror. The United States seemed to want to terrify the people of Vietnam, freeze them, make them stop, drive them back into their burrows, turn them to stone. (The anti-semite, Sartre has remarked, has a nostalgia for thingness, for the constancy of stone. One need not be anxious before stones; political philosophy becomes amenable to metaphors from physics.) Soon it appeared that, though our motives had once been mixed, the only conviction we wished finally to win Vietnamese hearts and minds over to was this: if they did thus and so, we would mutilate them. (Pacification: stillness: death.)

The United States' technique was not, as the Left sometimes said, genocide—to kill all—but rather terror: to kill some before the others, and so rule over the rest, over the audience turned to stone. There is a distinction to be drawn, I think, between the actions of terrorists—either the United States Army or terrorists who call themselves revolutionaries—and proletarian violence, at least as Marx imagined it. The terrorist does not want to do away with his audience; he wants some left to see, to control. Marx said the bourgeoisie—like the terrorists—must keep the workers alive, while torturing them, for it needed the workers for its own life. But the proletarian revolutionary could do away with the bourgeoisie utterly, it had no need of them. The proletarian does not need the bourgeois as audience; it does not wish to rule over him. And the proletarian or revolutionary does away with his own class as well—he brings his world to an end; "The revolutionary is a doomed man."

The United States wished to control and the means of control are logic, law, and terror. Vietnam was not merely America choosing terror for its means, but America making all these means seem, to many Americans, to be oddly related, almost interchangeable. (A lesson many countries, some on the left, some on the right, had already inscribed on its peoples' bodies.) As Roberto Unger wrote, "men come to believe that there is nothing in society that a will sufficiently violent cannot preserve or destroy. Thus legalism and terrorism, the commitment to rules, and the seduction of violence, are rival brothers, but brothers nonetheless."

This lesson *could* be read (why would one wish to read it so?): reason and law and terror are all means of control, and perhaps the ugliest of them is the basis of the rest. (Pascal wrote, "Not being able to make what was just strong, what was strong was made just.") This seemed to be the way our rulers felt and acted, had—it seemed—always acted. For every nuclear power is a terrorist holding the whole world in fear by holding any part of the world as hostage. Hiroshima, indeed any atomic tests, are demonstrations, spectacles of sacrifice, examples of what might happen to any who threaten the world order.

And the opposition—the terrorists—act from the same premises, from the same motives, as the rulers. If rule is terror on the government's part, terrorists use the same means against the rulers. Everyday now one reads in the newspaper, sees on television, or experiences for oneself, a world rocked by terror, ruled by it. Do we live many moments outside of the terror?

There have been hostages taken. Men and women and children are held at gunpoint. The terrorists are killed, the hostages are freed. Or the hostages are killed. Or both. Every day hostages are taken. Then reprisals are taken by the government to terrify the terrorists. (One knows who the authorities are because their actions are called "reprisals.") By 1974—one's hopefulness at an end—terror had become, it seemed, the substance of "revolutionary" politics. If you wanted to participate you had to be ready to pick up the gun, become a terrorist; ready to sacrifice others, sacrifice yourself. Those who weren't ready to join the action moved to the sidelines (to watch it on television).

The infant as described by Freud is faced by earthquakes, by times when his whole world is threatened with disruption, threatened by revolution from below—the upsurge of his own terrible vitality, his instincts, or id. The infant's ego feels that it will be overwhelmed, extinguished, its defenses shattered, its world dissolved. Usually in Freudian theory this danger is placed without. The child fears not its own instincts or its own vitality, but its parents' response to those instincts; he is terrified of what they will do to him.

But I think that we can understand terror better if we follow Norman O. Brown's revision of Freudian theory in *Life Against Death*. The ego's fantasies of retribution—fantasies of a primal crime, primal punishment, castration, fantasies of sexuality itself as a tale of crime and punishment—are its own ruses, its ways of controlling its own violence, its own unmanageable vitality.

To repress itself the child, made anxious by its own instincts, gives up a bit of itself, makes it alien, creates within itself on the basis of its fantasies the superego. It then represses its violence, its vitality, its instincts, in the service of the Master of the World, the angry and demanding god. That god requires that there be sacrifices on the child's part, a partial sacrifice of the instinct, a sacrifice of the loved object, and a symbolic sacrifice of the phallus. From this time on the phallus both does and does not belong to the male child—for it also belongs to god the father, a continual offering. A recurrent process is begun that will continue throughout the person's life: a phallus will be made and unmade, made and offered. In *Love's Body*, Brown sees this making and offering throughout culture, and in every act of sexual intercourse as well: "the rest of the body is to the penis as chorus to tragic hero, hypocritically and from a safe distance enjoying the thrill of being spectators at their own execution." The anxious ego has created a god to be appeased by sacrifices—for in this way the child need no longer, at least ostensibly, be afraid of his own internal power, no longer anxious before the id, before a violence that he was implicated in and that threatened to overwhelm him from within. Now he is afraid before the superego, the representative of "external power," an alien object, that can be placated momentarily by receiving partial sacrifices.

The sacrifices continue the process of protecting the ego against internal threats and the anxiety those threats create. It rids itself, in part, of the instinct by making a sacrifice of it, by directing its violence at a partial object, an object that is a part of the self, but not the self altogether. And the sacrifice not only appeases the god, it also terrifies the child—he himself is the real audience of his sacrifice. The ego demonstrates by its sacrifice its submission to the god and the necessity of its submission. By the sacrifice he represents to himself what might happen to himself in several senses. It is a sign for the total destruction that he is narrowly avoiding from the hands of the gods. What happens to the sacrifice is what might happen to him. It is a sign also for the total destruction he is narrowly avoiding from within; it reminds him of the true danger he is trying to avoid; so the horror of the sacrifice brings the activity of the body to a halt; the interplay of the instincts is brought to an end by danger; the body is turned to stone.

Thus, each one represses himself by terrifying himself.

The sacrifice one avoids is the sacrifice of the self, of the body and the world as it is. We avoid the sacrifice of the whole by the sacrifice of a part, and from this part sacrifice culture is built. "This piece of instinctual satisfaction which each person renounced," Freud wrote in "Civilized Sexual Morality," "was offered to the deity as a sacrifice, and the communal property thus acquired was declared sacred." And the culture thus created from these sacrifices is a way of continuing the sacrifice. Sacrifice is one means of repressing the self (terrorizing the self).

The sacrifice is the basis of government and its first purpose. Once it was the god that was sacrificed and the whole community by enacting the rite enacted its own cyclic dissolution. "Cosmos has become chaos again," Jan Kott writes of this ceremony, "so that everything can begin anew." Then the king is substituted for the god; the god rises from the stage, watching the sacrifice; and the community becomes an audience to the rite. Next the king chooses a substitute victim to die for him, a member of the chorus who becomes identified with king, chorus, and god, at the moment of death. Through the victim we enjoy an identity with the divine, release from guilt, and the thrill of being spectators at our own execution. We survive our death.

The god has risen off stage, external to us, as we have receded from the king and become an audience. "In the first row of seats," Kott writes in his essay on *The Bacchae,* "stood the famous throne of Dionysus, the reserved seat of the god. In other Dionysian theaters . . . the mask of the god was hung on the proscenium columns. Dionysus was a spectator of *The Bacchae.*" The god watches; the audience watches; the community does not enter into chaos; theater is born. "The ritual" Kott writes, "has turned into ritual murder. Brecht wrote in his 'Little Organon': 'Theater may be said to be derived from ritual, but that is only to say that it becomes theater once the two have separated.' " The king is now our intermediary, our priest, offering a sacrifice. Theater is born—"History," Kott says, "has been unleashed."

The sacrifice is a partial sacrifice, a way of avoiding the total sacrifice, a way of avoiding entering the chaos, and giving up the world as it is—one's habitual ways of ordering the world, one's defenses, one's personality. It is this sense of sacrifice that underlies Séjourne's book on the Aztecs, *Burning Water.* To explain the extreme cruelty of the human sacrifices required by the Aztecs, Séjourne argues that the original inhabitants of the area whom the Aztecs conquered had practiced a quite different kind of sacrifice. These people, the Toltecs, had a sacrifice of the self: a surrender of the ego, "a mystic union with the divinity which the individual could achieve only through successive steps, and after a life of contemplation and penitence." This religious, mystical sense of sacrifice was perverted by the Aztec conquerors, who changed it into an ideology of literal human sacrifice, an ideology suitable for rule, government, for imperialism. Toltec sacrifice became for the Aztecs, "a low witch-craft: the material transmission of human energy to the sun. The exalted revelation of the eternal unity spirit was converted into a principle of cosmic anthrophagy. The liberation of the individual, the separate 'I', came to be understood with crude literalness only, and achieved through literal killings, which in their turn fomented wars." The necessity for sacrifice created the need for wars; these wars provided victims ("Dainties, hot and fresh from the field of battle") to feed the sun; such wars and sacrifices were also a means of rule, for to carry them out terrified the populace and required the totalitarian rule of the chiefs.

There is a parallel to this, I think, in the war in Vietnam. In order to insure the continued prosperity and productiveness of monopoly capitalism, there must be war. That is: there must be victims to feed the machines, there must be waste, sacrifices (to kill someone in Vietnam was to "waste" them). These sacrifices also help to keep the structure of the world as it is; the necessities of war block alternative organizations from being considered; they prevent that catastrophe to the system foretold by Marx—the sun going out. In any case, the story of the Aztecs and the Toltecs is a story of the beginning of history; spiritual sacrifice becomes literal sacrifice, or terror. Terror is here the basis of government. The Aztec citizen, like the child, is faced with a "tragic dilemma" that "obliges him to choose between indulging in a massacre or bringing about the end of the world," the end of our world as we know it. There must be sacrifice of others instead of the whole community entering chaos; sacrifice of others instead of self-sacrifice. "History has been unleashed."

But it is not necessary for the Aztecs to pervert the pure Toltec creed. Each human child betrays himself.

Another turn of the knife: sacrifice itself is now one of the ways the world is ordered. It is a manner of defense, and like any defense, it is part of our character. But now one acts to maintain that character as it is; one acts by sacrifice to maintain the necessity for sacrifice, world without end. "The adult ego," Freud wrote, "finds itself compelled to seek out those situations in reality which can serve as an approximate substitute for the original danger, so as to be able to justify in relation to them its maintaining its habitual modes of reaction."

But the sacrifice itself always reminds one of the original source of anxiety, the real danger, the one that the self is implicated in, that is within. The anxiety means that new sacrifices are required; the king, the ego, is never secure; there must be never-ending sacrifice. ("Christ," Pascal wrote, "is in agony until the end of the world.")

Never-ending sacrifice; or therapy. Once wrongdoers were immediately killed. Then, according to Frazier, the criminal became a substitute for the king in the sacrifice. Now the criminal is "rehabilitated," that is, therapy replaces execution; the state, the king, makes the prisoner a continuous show for the rest of society, for the ego. (When Bakhunin tried to imagine the anarchist world—the world without representative government—he contended that the criminal would be excluded from the community. If he tried to reenter, anyone could kill him. At least in Bakhunin there are no privileged executioners, and no continuous performances.)

Continuous sacrifice—but the instinct is not gratified, it has not achieved its end. So the sacrifices must express both the self's submission to the god, and one's continual restless discontent, one's anger. The sacrifice is also useless industrial production: waste, trash, rotten goods. And the self is guilty for its anger at the god. There must be further sacrifices. (Therefore, as Herbert Mullins, the prophet of Jonah, said, "we will always have murder.")

Now, whenever there is political killing no matter what the motive named, I look for the theater of sacrifice: the infant described by Freud, the madman making an offering to stop the earthquake.

The terrorist may speak more sensibly than Herbert Mullins, in a syntax we are accustomed to (its origins now forgotten). He allows his bombs to dismember his victims, rather than personally performing that surgery. He speaks not of "the Prophecy of Jonah," but in the accents of contract law, quid pro quo, the logic of history. He makes demands, he wants his target to do something, or cease from doing something. He threatens (as he has been threatened, as we are all constantly threatened, or threaten ourselves). It is the same threat always: if you don't do what I say then I will kill this representative, this person who might be you (who, by the magic of sacrifice, becomes you when he is killed).

Yet behind these words I hear Herbert Mullins, possessed by voices that are singing "the die song." For if the ego, if our reality, is our collective creation, is social, then there is no escape from the breakup of our society, no high ground. The ego of the terrorist, though it speaks as if on the side of the masses, as if trying to hasten this dissolution, is also, I think, suffering this dissolution. But he is suffering it far more acutely, more desperately, more sensitively, and his anxiety is the greater. And the terrorist, no matter how he names his acts, is trying to gain control of himself, stop the anxiety, stop the dissolution.

The terrorist speaks of acting *for* the masses. The power within the terrorist (for "the masses" are one's power projected) is made by the terrorist absolutely external to himself, made into an idol, a god. (The revolutionary, Che Guevara wrote, in "Man and Socialism in Cuba," must make the masses his most hallowed image. It must substitute for all the life he denies himself.) Like the child, like Herbert Mullins, by making sacrifices he will appease the god that he himself has created. (As in *Man's Fate:* "Ch'en was becoming aware, with a revulsion verging on nausea, that he stood here not as a fighter, but as a sacrificial priest. He was serving the god of his choice.")

The masses that are within him become something external to him, an inversion of themselves, a god that demands sacrifices. They become "the image of the masses," speaking with one voice, demanding blood. Rosa Luxembourg, in describing the actions of terrorist revolutionaries in Russia, describes this process: "The ego . . . takes revenge in its revolutionary dream world by placing itself on the throne and declaring itself to be all powerful—as a conspiratorial committee acting in the name of a non-existent people's will." The People's Will is a vengeful god, an exacting one, but such a god can be placated by the proper obsessive and difficult acts.

The Indian terrorist group, the Naxalites, in their degeneration, show forth the image of what is always there in terrorism:

> It is the theory of Vijay Tendulkar, the Marathix playwright . . . that
> Naxalism, as it developed in Bengal, became confused with the Kali
> cult: Kali "the black one," the coal black aboriginal goddess, surviving
> in Hinduism as the emblem of female destructiveness, garlanded with
> human skulls, tongue forever out for fresh blood, eternally sacrificed
> to but insatiable. Many of the Naxalite killings in Bengal . . . had a
> ritualistic quality. Maoism was used only to define the sacrifice. Certain
> people—not necessarily rich and powerful—might be deemed "class
> enemies." Initiates would then be bound to the cause—of Kali, of
> Naxalism—by being made to witness the killing of these class enemies
> and dipping their hands in the blood.

As Kott says, on the historical stage (where divine time and historical
time appear to have separated, when the god has risen from the stage
and is outside us) "ritual has turned into ritual murder." Ritual
murder has become slaughter.

As with the child, or with Herbert Mullins, the sacrifice insures
that the terrorist will be spared from the dissolution, the death of the
world. By the act he stands not in the present anymore, but in his
goal, in the future, at the end of the process; he has retained himself
as he is in this future (been catapulted into it); he is at the end of
time, but unchanged.

He has made an offering to the god, so he will be part of the
saving remnant, the elect, the Party, the revolutionary leadership;
this feeling of being saved can coexist with great actual danger, for
it is not actual danger that he is battling, but something that is
happening within him. "Few people," Edgar Z. Friedenberg writes,
"will accept much increase in anxiety, but most will accept quite a
lot of fear—an infinite amount if the situation is arranged so that
anxiety diminishes as fear increases . . . Because the soldier's self-
image is linked to his unit, and to his image of himself as morally
courageous, he will become more anxious if he abandons his buddies,
and seeks safety, and less anxious if he goes into battle on their
side." In intensifying his actual danger, the terrorist is also intensifying his sense of self, of his own identity.

The power that the terrorist wants to be saved from is the
power that is within him, the dissolution that is happening to him,
the real power of the masses, as it is felt within the person. "Social-

ism," Sorel remarks, "has always inspired terror because of the enormous element of the unknown it contains. People would feel that a transformation of this kind would permit no turning back." Faced with this transformation (though faced is not the right word, for it implies an external force) the terrorist, too, is afraid. And the terrorist's choice of action reveals where he feels the real danger to be. For his action separates him from the masses, rather than plunging him into them (or opening him to them within himself). "Man does not become man again," Brecht wrote of the true communist, "by stepping forth from the masses, but by sinking deeper into them." But it is this plunge, this sacrifice of self ("the revolutionary is a doomed man"), that the terrorist resists by his actions. The terrorist, in the name of his god, his hallowed image, rises from the masses that Brecht speaks of, distances and separates himself from them. (*Man's Fate:* "There were millions of lives and all now rejected his; but what was their wretched condemnation beside death.") The terrorist acts as a priest, doing what he has decided must be done (he hears the voice of his god, singing the die song), what the masses, the audience, wouldn't dare to do. He becomes their representative.

Terrorist action is never, by its nature, the shared action that Marx imagined. There is a resemblance to be remarked between the parliamentarian described by Sorel in his *Reflections on Violence,* and the terrorist:

> if by chance our Parliamentary socialists get possession of the reins of government they will prove to be worthy successors of the inquisition. . . . We might again see the state triumphing by the hand of the executioner.
>
> Proletarian acts of violence have no resemblance to these proscriptions; they are purely and simply acts of war . . . Everything in war is carried out without hatred and without the spirit of revenge; in war the vanquished are not killed; non-combatants are not made to bear the consequences of the disappointments which the armies may have experienced . . . : force is then displayed according to its own nature, without ever professing to borrow anything from the judicial proceedings which society sets up against criminals.

The link between terrorist and parliamentarian is not simply their bloodthirstiness, but rather the feature they share, the feature that Sorel is pointing to, that they are *representatives*. They act for others; they concentrate power in their own hands; and the cruelty, the spectacle, the acting out of the forbidden, is part of the process by which the distinction between representative and mass is established, by which power is concentrated and audience created.

By performing terrorist acts the terrorist lifts himself away from the masses, escapes them, attempts—like the parliamentarian described by Sorel—to stand outside that unknown process that is his death, the transformation of the world from which there is no turning back. He becomes a leader. Charles Manson had a revolutionary theory not a great deal different perhaps from Blanquis's or from John Brown's—or from Lenin's praxis. (Or perhaps we should say that Manson's actions illuminate for us—as the psychopathology of everyday life does for our daily activities—what is present but hidden in those more respectable theories.) The killing of Sharon Tate and her friends by Manson's followers would be a signal to black people to rise up and kill whites in the cities. Manson and his disciples would have retreated to safety, away from these masses during the bloodbath, by going into the desert in dune buggies, to return after the destruction when Manson would be crowned King. Though the masses are here allowed to perform some of the killing, they recognize that it is the leader, who by the sacrifices he offered, gave the signal, overcame the taboo, and is entitled by virtue of that signal, that first blood, to lead.

Terrorist action, unlike the revolutionary actions of the proletariat that Marx foresaw, does not, cannot, abolish its own necessity. Like the parliamentarian described by Sorel, the terrorist requires a constant procession of sacrifices, scapegoats, of examples, of threats to his power, his defenses, that must be put down. Terrorist action does not foresee its own end within the act (as the actions of Marx's proletarians do). The terrorist, by his act, only changes places with his oppressor, changes seats, makes the ruler into an audience; he does not do away with him (and certainly not in a dialectical process that would also do away with himself). The terrorist makes the ruler fear; terrifies him, has power over him, turns him into stone. The terrorist, like the parliamentarian, needs the whole structure; he needs the theater. There must be fear in the ruling classes, but no one must go so far as to end the system of representation.

The terrorist, like the child, must split himself in his actions, must watch them. For he is anxious before the id, before his own vitality (which is the end of this world) and wants to convert that anxiety to fear—fear of something external to him. The victim is a demonstration to himself of what he imagines he must fear—his own destruction at the hands of his god, the masses, History—if he were not taking this action, and so placating that imaginary god. It also unites him with "the masses" in their new vengeful guise (as the worker by the continual sacrifice of himself in labor is united with his alienated power).

The terrorist's sacrifice places him outside the process of the revolution, at its end, safe from change and its anxiety. The terrorist has turned himself to stone, "sequestered his own vitality." As in Lenin's theory of the Party structure, he is an underground man; buried; in the grave. In the most horrifying and literal sense he has fulfilled Nechayev's dictum, "The revolutionary is a doomed man." The doomed man is a dead man.

We deal with our inward violence, with the dissolution of our world by making a show for ourselves, by terrifying ourselves with that show. A terrorist, then, is a joint creation for this task, a priest, or antichrist—"a scapegoat, a kill crazy homo-sapien bull." The society sings the die song to him—and he makes the sacrifice, commits the murder, helping us turn (or try to turn for we never succeed) our anxiety into terror.

We seem even to have learned to take a certain pleasure in these shows of sacrifice and waste. By 1974 our movies were often enormous spectacles of disaster—sinking ocean liners, earthquakes devastating cities, exploding airships, bombs placed on luxury liners, fires in skyscrapers. The tragic sense debased becomes a voluptuous pleasure in one's own terror, the Romantic Agony, "the beauty of the Medusa's Head" or "—the tempestuous loveliness of terror," as Shelley names it—the pleasure of watching, vicariously participating in the scenarios of sadomasochism, of partial self-destruction, of sacrifice, the pleasure of being terrified, of being turned to stone.

Patty Hearst falling in love with her kidnappers (or our decision that she had since this was the story we delighted in imagining) is one figure who illustrates pleasure in terror, the pleasure of being with the god who destroys us (but only a little at a time), the god who keeps us terrified. (Rilke: "Beauty's nothing but the beginning of terror we're still just able to bear/and why we adore it so is because it serenely disdains to destroy us.") It is as if now we have collaborated in the creation of the god so that we might have both the terror and the pleasure-in-terror of submission. The radical movement in the late 1960s was, like Patty Hearst, in love with a gunman, in love with figures from the Third World, armed revolutionaries, Brown Berets, Black Panther gunmen. Love and dread became for this world nearly indistinguishable. ("Dread," Kierkegaard wrote in his *Journal*, "is the desire for what one fears, a sympathetic antipathy; dread is an alien power which takes hold of the individual and yet one cannot extricate oneself from it, does not wish to, because one is afraid, but what one fears attracts one.")

There is a tendency to take a certain *pleasure* in watching our destruction—the scene of execution in which one identifies with the sacrifice. The child watching the primal scene (a scene he sees or imagines, and sees distorted by his imaginings) is the child terrifying himself and enjoying a pleasurable fear. The child wishing to return to the womb (and so overcome the trauma of being born, the anxiety caused by separation, of being apart from the mother, of being overwhelmed by the instincts, of dying) identifies with the phallus, with the father's penis, the penis that can—partially, symbolically—return to the womb. (Pentheus wishing to see his mother's ecstasy climbs a tall fir. "Pentheus is defenseless against the temptation to return to the womb," Kott writes. "Dionysus: 'You will be carried home—' Pentheus: 'O luxury.' Dionysus: Cradled in your mother's arms.'")

But in this identification the child is both gratified and terrified at once, for the penis is also an offering, a sacrifice. In the primal scene the mother is eating the father's penis. The primal scene hallucinated by the anxious child terrifies him, turns him to stone. Again and again throughout his life he will recreate this scene of sacrifice, making and offering a phallus, trying to recreate as viewer—but only as viewer—both this scene's vicarious satisfaction and effective self-repression.

The child watching the primal scene is one metaphor for how history is made now, and how we participate in it vicariously. And this is true not only for the television watchers but for the participants. The radical movement, or much of it, was formed, like terrorism, at anxiety over death—the imagined death of our country, the death of the imperial ego, a death all felt and tried to delight in. Political actions were "demonstrations": events to be watched, and thereby spectral events even for their participants. The *real* life of these events, their political meaning was when they were seen by others on television or read about in the newspapers. Mass rallies are an example—the point was the number of people present: the real life of the event was in the count reported by the newspapers.

These actions were events to be watched; the actors identify with the imagined audience: they are viewers watching. These were revolutionary actions in which the world was destroyed, the participants transformed—but they were only watching, and so not really destroyed. Really, one is saved. Like gay Tom Sawyers, one can watch one's own funeral. To be watching the destruction of one's own country—by throwing a rock through a store window (it was called trashing)—was to be outside that destruction, an observer; it was to commit suicide and survive it. The feeling that one was watching was itself the indication that one was part of the elect, on the side of History, *saved.*

Patty Hearst, combining in one figure both the terrorist and the victim, is the type for all of us. It is as if she were one of the readers of *The San Francisco Chronicle* watching the Patty Hearst story (just as in the late 1960s we thought we were watching the Fall of America). To be terrified, like the child watching the primal scene is to be stiff, dead—to reassure oneself by that feeling that one is not a participant but an observer, an observer of one's own (but only symbolic) destruction; terrified and exhilarated at once; destroyed and saved.

For even when terrorists act they are watching themselves;

their actions are spectacles. Again, the Symbionese Liberation Army provided the extreme trope for this. Each day their poses became more and more grotesque as they turned themselves into caricatures to insure that they would hold the attention of the television cameras, until finally they could watch themselves being burnt up on television in Los Angeles, even as they were being physically burnt up. (It was live action.) Our recent history seems to indicate that there is a giddy, finally maddening sense of immortality that comes from being on television. To see oneself on television is to feel that one is surviving the fire even as it consumes one.

And in the 1960s, the left was almost in love with the process of making offerings, putting its hand in the fire, sacrificing itself, holding demonstrations in which one faced tactical police, onanistic scenarios in which "a child is being beaten." To love one's own guilt to the point where one enjoys making sacrifices, enjoys the punitive actions one performs for the superego, is to eroticize one's destruction, one's death. If the superego is formed during the child's homosexual phase, the relations between superego and ego are libidinal, and the harsh dictates of conscience, the sacrifices, the being beaten are libidinized. People in this situation create what Freud called "the pure culture of the death instinct," an erotic sacrificial offering of oneself and of substitutes for oneself. (Weathermen at one point discussed killing white babies.) Love and dread have become the same.

And these pages too are like those actions, a delight in terror, a way of scaring others, and scaring myself. I would like to speak directly, to speak violence (this "vital death," as Augustine calls it). I think violence shows forth in metaphor—in which each object is yoked to something unlike itself, and so fused, burnt up. But violence never appears in my words for they are words of analysis, words that attempt reflection—an activity of the ego, the self looking backwards, trying to bring enlightenment, being a therapist, constituting itself as if outside the process. Even to *admire* violence (as if it could be admired) is to have the masochistic, totally illusory pleasure of being present at one's own funeral. I want, I think, to say violence, but I show only terror.

And the people, withdrawing to the sidelines to watch the spectacle, face each other not as part of the mass, but each one alone, each with his vision of the others distorted by the terror process. Each makes of the other a suitable sacrifice. I make every other a projection of my own violence, a violence that still fills me with anxiety when I see it in your face. I see your face through that anxiety as the face of a monster. I hope by sacrificing you to diminish what makes me anxious—"the next man is one too many"—to turn my anxiety into fear. For to see you killed is a terrible thing, but it is better than the anxiety that I feel before you. The more I am terrified, the less I will recognize the violence within, the more I repress it, the less like you I am, and so, the less danger to myself.

It is "the signal of anxiety" that is necessary for this process of transformation to begin. The signal can be seen in the way that the media project a distorted image of anyone who might shake this order, turn them to grotesques, suitable sacrifices. (The media are not simply an imposition, a method of someone else's propaganda, but a way for society to think out loud, to manage itself.) The press is the example Freud uses in *Inhibitions, Symptoms and Anxiety* to illustrate the workings of anxiety:

> We are apt to think of the ego as powerless against the id, but when it is opposed to an instinctual pleasure in the id it has only to give the signal of unpleasure in order to obtain its object with the aid of that almost omnipotent institution, the pleasure principle. To take this situation by itself for a moment we can illustrate it by an example from another field. Let us imagine a certain country in which a small faction objects to a proposed measure, the passage of which would have the support of the masses. This minority obtains command of the press, and by its help manipulates the supreme arbiter "public" opinion" and so succeeds in preventing the measure from being passed.

The media, a part of our collective ego, turns the face of the other into an unchanging mask, a grotesque, a metaphor become stone and, if they want to be noticed they collaborate in this process; the rebel wears a clownish costume, a terrible mask.

We turn our power to grotesques, and, scared of each other, of our own possibilities, our now terrifying future, we turn against each other, we rend each other. (Late one night a young man called to tell me that he had planted a bomb in my house, a drunken voice, vicious, insistent, "This isn't a wrong number, you fucker. There's a bomb in your house that will go off in ten minutes." There was no bomb, I knew; the newspapers had been full of bombings recently. There was no bomb, though I saw myself as an image in the movie *Juggernaut,* being blown upward off the earth. It was just a random call; they would come now and kill us. The doors are glass, there's no way to lock them. They were already watching . . . My girlfriend's sixteen-year-old brother received a phone call each day after school, a voice that said over and over, "I'm going to kill you." My sister, in Boston, received calls from a boy who said that he was Charles Manson's brother, that he had dozens of guns and explosives, and was going to kill her.)

"At this stage," Sartre writes, "they are cornered between our guns pointing at them and those terrifying compulsions, those desires for murder which spring from the depths of their spirits . . . If this suppressed fury does not find an outlet it turns in a vacuum and devastates the oppressed creatures themselves. In order to free themselves they even massacred each other." But we have created the guns pointing at us; they are our gods; we must make them an offering; we turn and rend each other.

The end of the play: the torn fragments cannot be reassembled.

"BURNING
THE
CHRISTMAS
GREENS";
OR, DESPAIR

1974

Friday night I was sitting with friends watching the television news. It was eleven-thirty. I remember that it was drafty, that I felt a chill around my legs—perhaps because houses in California were built for balmier weather; or because Pacific Gas and Electric had changed the pressure at which gas was sent. In any case, I couldn't seem to get warm enough. The house didn't have a fireplace.

The news was about the kidnapping of Patricia Hearst. Randolph Hearst read a statement that he had already given two million dollars for food for the poor and couldn't afford to give more, as the kidnappers now insisted. The matter was, he said, "out of his hands." He went back through the wide doors of his house, and closed them behind him. A sepulchral looking spokesman for the Hearst Corporation, a man with a face like a mealy potato, said the corporation would give four million dollars, but, he added—perhaps to forestall further demands by the kidnappers—Randolph Hearst didn't control the corporation, and they weren't going to give a penny more.

A newsman went on to talk about the food giveaway plan that the kidnappers had required. It was already under way, he said, in the bay area, particularly in East Oakland, whose ravaged storefronts and bleak streets were shown to us as he talked. The local Hearst newspaper, the *Examiner,* had said that the Hearst family had received a vast number of small contributions from the very people the SLA had named as the "Benefactors" of the kidnapping—the poor of California. And the paper reported receiving thousands of letters from the poor; all but one of them had said they wanted nothing to do with extorted food—they'd rather go hungry.

In East Oakland, before the food center had opened, five

thousand people crowded the streets surrounding the storefront. They were a crowd of black people—East Oakland is a black neighborhood—many of them women with children, and young black men, the kind one often saw in the late 1960s at support demonstrations for the Black Panthers. One might see a young man, say, at the edge of the crowd, not sure how he felt about the Panthers, whether with so many white people involved the Panthers could be trusted. His clothes would be colorful, but not expensive or flashy. He might be wearing a knitted stocking cap. He would walk with a slight slouch, not beaten down, but coiled, wary. He looked obviously dangerous—which was, no doubt, how he wanted to look.

The cameraman moved in for a close-up of a fat black woman. There was a lot of shouting at the newscaster. He asked the woman how she felt about taking extorted food, and she replied, looking into the camera, "I'm very sorry for that young lady. But I have a family to feed. I need that food." There was a terrible bold assertiveness to her voice.

The truck came with the food, and the crowd began to push towards it, shoving each other, thousands of hands reaching up towards the back of the truck. The people on the truck began to hurl the packages into the crowd. The newscaster said that many of the people, insulted by the way the food was tossed to them, threw it back into the truck. Then the Tactical Police moved in, pushing the crowd back, and occasionally knocking one of the black men down and hitting him on the head.

Then there were the usual news stories about the gas shortage and the long lines outside filling stations.

After the news someone in the room spoke of a visit from his college roommate, now in the Venceremos Brigade—a radical group based in Palo Alto. As his roommate left, he had said, on the way out, "You won't be able to buy guns as long as you think. You should get a handgun now, and a shotgun." And he told my friend what make and caliber to get. (Arrogant talk—as if Venceremos members had some special knowledge; the Party's wisdom about the "logic of history"—simple-minded talk, given the complexities of our difficulty.) My friend went on to talk about how some day we'd have to hike over to see our friends—the automobile by then defunct—

and stay for a few days at a time. He said that in a way the news made him jolly. I knew that pleasure myself, the delight, the savage lightheadedness of a protected nihilism.

I was reminded of Stubb, the second mate in *Moby-Dick*. After the first day's chase of the whale, one of the stoved boats is dragged up on the main deck. Stubb, eyeing the wreck, exclaimed, "The thistle the ass refused; it pricked his mouth too keenly sir; ha ha!"

And Ahab replies, "What soulless thing is this that laughs before a wreck? Man, man! did I not know thee brave as fearless fire, (and as mechanical) I could swear thou wert a poltroon. Groan nor laugh should be heard before a wreck."

Most of the time I am a Stubb myself. The room in which we were watching television was scattered about with toys, like underground comics and fancy kaleidoscopes, to pass the time with. As William Carlos Williams writes, in "Burning the Christmas Greens":

> At the thick of the dark
> the moment of the cold's
> deepest plunge we brought branches
> cut from the green trees
>
> to fill our need, and over
> doorways, about paper Christmas
> bells covered with tinfoil
> and fastened by red ribbons
>
> we stuck the green prongs
> in the windows hung
> woven wreaths and above pictures
> the living green. On the
>
> mantle we built a green forest
> and among those hemlock
> sprays put a herd of small
> white deer as if they
>
> were walking there. All this!
> and it seemed gentle and good
> to us.

As my kaleidoscope and comic books and drugs seemed good. In college, when we were occupying buildings and bringing down the government, I was happy to be alive in such an exciting time. The world was watching; we were the local Vietcong. Then the country was at war, and prosperous. Now, conditions, by not changing, slowly grow worse. I no longer know which building to occupy. The news I watch isn't about me. My legs get cold at night, the pictures on the screen are sometimes like a gun pointed at my head, and I wish I were alive in a different time. And if now is the time for burning the Christmas greens? Fire is, Williams says, no toy; it is dangerous, coiled, painful. As in *Paterson:*

> Fire burns; that is the first law.
> When a wind fans it the flames
>
> are carried abroad. Talk
> fans the flames. They have
>
> manoeuvred it so that to write
> is a fire and not only of the blood.
> . . . .
>   The writing
> should be a relief,
>
> relief from the conditions
> which as we advance become—a fire,
>
> a destroying fire. For the writing
> is also an attack and means must be
>
> found to scotch it—at the root
> if possible. So that
>
> to write, nine tenths of the problem
> is to live.

That man in the bright stocking cap was a fire, and that fat woman who needed food was a fire—and those thousands of arms that reached up, each of those raised arms, those taut hands.

When I saw Randolph Hearst say it was out of his hands, in front of the big wood doors of his house, I didn't believe him. But, I realized, I had made it hard for myself to imagine what Hearst was thinking, feeling. That stout woman did not imagine what Hearst was thinking, and did not, despite her words, care particularly about that poor young woman, his daughter. (And I wonder what I would have to do to imagine what that woman was thinking?) If I were to talk to one of those dangerous black men we would not trust each other, and would have no language in common. (As it says in *Paterson*: "The language, the language / fails them / They do not know the words.") There are doors, there are boundaries between us, and those boundaries could as much as anything, destroy our imagination of each other, and so destroy our nation. As Williams writes in "Asphodel," "It is difficult / to get the news from poems / yet men die miserably every day / for lack / of what is found there." But what is found there, he says, is fire.

In *Paterson* Williams welcomes that fire, invokes it, fire,

Of which we drink and are drunk and in the end
are destroyed (as we feed). But the flames
are flames with a requirement, a belly of their
own that destroys . . . .
. . . .
                              Papers
(consumed) scattered to the winds. Black
The ink burned white, metal white. So be it.
Come overall beauty. Come soon. So be it.
. . . .
                    An iron dog, eyes
aflame in flame-filled corridor. A drunkenness
of flames. So be it. A bottle, mauled
by the flames, belly-bent with laughter:
yellow, green. So be it—of drunkenness
survived, in guffaws of flame. All fire afire!
So be it. Swallowing the fire. So be
it. . . .
                    Chortling at flames
sucked in, a multiformity of laughter, a
flaming gravity surpassing the sobriety of
flames, a chastity of annihilation. Recreant,
calling it good. Calling the fire good.
So be it. The beauty of the fire-blasted sand

that was glass, that was a bottle: unbottled
Unabashed. So be it.

And the library of Paterson, too, is burned up, destroyed,
"BECAUSE IT IS SILENT, IT / IS SILENT BY DEFECT OF VIRTUE IN THAT
IT / CONTAINS NOTHING OF YOU."

And because it contains nothing of that black woman with
her big belly, her family. (But even as I say that, I am embarrassed,
reminding myself of the polemics of the thirties—as if what is called
for is proletarian art. No, she is in the library, and there is something
in there for her which would nourish her. But she has, apparently, a
more pressing need for a more ordinary kind of food, and there are
boundaries between her and the nourishment the library will contain.
It is in the fire of those boundaries, those high closed doors, that the
library in *Paterson* is destroyed.)

Williams calls this burning the Christmas greens. If one is to
survive one must, he says, find a will to burn them. And that is also,
Williams writes, burning the cross—burning the true cross as well as
the false. (Is the true cross, Williams asks, that which doesn't burn,
survives the fire, or that which burns most brightly, pentecostal?)

Williams burns the cross, "a woman's world of crossed sticks,
stopping thought," as he calls it in "To Daphne and Virginia":

> The mind is the cause of our distresses
>   but of it we can build anew.
>   Oh something more than
> it flies off to:
>   a woman's world,
>   of crossed sticks, stopping
> thought. A new world
>   is only a new mind.

"A new world is only a new mind." A new mind here is a
mind that is passing through fire, that is on fire. As Roy Harvey
Pearce wrote, in "Williams and the New Mode":

> He would have the poem be the means whereby subject and object are
> fused. Towards this purpose he has directed the bulk of his poems
> since *Paterson*. He was, in fact, moving towards it at the time he was

working towards Paterson. There is "Choral: The Pink Church" in which we read:

> *"Sing!*
> *transparent to the light*
>   *through which the light*
> *shines, through the stone,*
>   *until*
> *the stone-light glows,*
>   *pink jade*
> *—that is the light and is*
>   *a stone*
> *and is a church—if the image*
>   *hold . . ."*

"The Pink Church" is the poet's world, and all the persons, places and things it contains; much of the poem runs Whitman like over their names, so attempting to absorb them into that ultimate pinkness, that ultimate light, that ultimate revelation, into which a full sense of their presence must issue. Likewise there is "Burning the Christmas Greens," which begins:

> *"Their time past, pulled down*
> *cracked and flung to the fire*
> *—go up in a roar*
>
> *All recognition lost, burnt clean*
> *clean in the flame, the green*
> *dispersed, a living red,*
> *flame red, red as blood wakes*
> *on the ash—"*

Again that light which moves as the blood moves. The theme of the poem is put explicitly towards the end:

> *"Transformed!"*

A new world then is a new mind, a mind transformed—subject and object fused. This is what the ecologist, Gregory Bateson, speaks of in his *Steps to An Ecology of Mind:*

> If you put God outside, and set him vis-à-vis his creation and if you have the idea that you are created in his image, you will logically . . . see yourself as outside and against the things around you . . .

If this is your estimate of your relation to nature . . . your
likelihood of survival will be that of a snowball in hell . . .

If I am right, the whole of our thinking about what we are,
and what other people are has got to be restructured. . . . The most
important task today is, perhaps, to learn to think in the new way . . .
I don't know how to think that way . . . if I am cutting down a tree
I still think "Gregory Bateson" is cutting down a tree. *I* am cutting
down the tree . . .

There are experiences . . . which may help me to imagine
what it would be like to have the habit of correct thought. . . . I have
experienced . . . the disappearance of the division between self and the
music to which I was listening. The perceiver and the thing perceived
became strangely united into a single entity . . .

The poets have known these things all through the ages, but
the rest of us have gone astray into all sorts of false reifications of the
"self" and the separations between the "self" and "experience."

So to survive, he says, requires a new mind, where "subject and object are fused," where there is no "reified self," no
"division between self and the music to which I was listening."
One must become, then, like the hero of *Paterson*, who says, "Why
even speak of 'I' . . . which/interests me almost not at all." Otherwise we will see "ourselves as outside and against the things around
us," and we will, Bateson writes, "die either of the toxic by-products
of our own hate, or simply, of over-population and overgrazing.
The raw materials of the world are finite."

A new mind, where subject and object are fused also, in
Williams's work, invokes a fire:

> —Transformed!
>
> Violence leaped and appeared.
> Recreant! roared to life
> as the flame rose through and
> our eyes recoiled from it.

"Our eyes recoiled from it," Williams warns, recoil from
the breaking of boundaries, the violence of that fire. One hopes
then, that Williams old, in "Asphodel," is right:

> Inseparable from the fire
>   its light
>
>   takes precedence over it.

Then follows
        what we have dreaded—
                but it can never
overcome what has gone before.
        In the hugh gap
                between the flash
and the thunderstroke
        spring has come in
                or a deep snow fallen.

TWENTY-TWO (BROKEN) NOTES ON SAMUEL BECKETT

1. Closing Time: to put an end to all this, *Endgame*, or the end of the world. Closing time as Beckett's revolutionary project: to close time, "to shut up shop, dappy" (as it says in *Finnegans Wake*).

2. "Closing time": a description Joyce and Beckett each thought, with their own inflection, of where we are now ("Time, Gentlemen, please?") and of how things go (around) in circles, Vico's circles, or Nietzsche's circles of eternal recurrence, or Joyce's circles of "commodious vicus of recirculation." A circling world of purgatory, going nowhere over and over. Samuel Beckett describes Joyce's vision:

> In what sense, then is Mr. Joyce's work purgatorial? In the absolute absence of the Absolute. Hell is the static lifelessness of unrelieved viciousness. Paradise is the static lifelessness of unrelieved immaculation. Purgatory a flood of movement and vitality released by the conjunction of these two elements. There is a continuous purgatorial process at work, in the sense that the vicious circle of humanity is being achieved. . . .On this earth that is purgatory . . . the machine proceeds. And no more than this; neither prize nor penalty; simply a series of stimulants to enable the kitten to catch its own tail. And the partially purgatorial agent? The partially purged.

Beckett describes *Finnegans Wake* or history—a kitten chasing its own tail, an infernal machine—no, *not* infernal, but purgatorial, "our wholemole millwheeling viccoclometer" with humanity caught in or on or as its gears, going round and round forever, getting nowhere.

3.   A world of eternal recurrence, Nietzsche wrote, could be the source of our greatest pleasure or of our greatest despair:

> *The greatest stress.* How if some . . . night a demon were to sneak after you into your loneliest loneliness and say to you, "This life as you now live it and have lived it, you will have to live once more and innumerable times more; and there will be nothing new in it, but every pain and every joy and every thought and sigh . . . must return to you —all in the same succession and sequence— . . ." If this thought were to gain possession of you, it would change you, as you are, or perhaps crush you. The question in each and every thing "Do you want this once more and innumerable times more?" would weigh upon your actions as the greatest stress. Or how well disposed would you have to become to your self and to life to crave nothing more fervently than this ultimate confirmation eternal and seal?

This recurrence, this eternal recurrence, in this world, filled Nietzsche's Zarathustra with nausea. This nausea must be confronted in all of Beckett's works:

> The patients were described as "cut off" from reality, from the rudimentary blessings of the laymen's reality . . . . The function of treatment was to bridge the gulf, to translate the sufferer from his own pernicious little private dungheap to the glorious world of discrete particulars, where it would be his inestimable prerogative once again to wonder, love, hate, desire, rejoice and howl in a reasonable balanced manner, and comfort himself with the society of others in the same predicament.
>
> All this was duly revolting to Murphy.

René Clair said that if a film were made of a man's day— a film that was exactly as long as that day, that was that day in every detail—and then the film were shown to that man, the man would go mad watching it. (Nietzsche warns, "If this thought were to gain possession of you, it would change you as you are, or perhaps crush you.") Why don't we go mad?

> Vladimir: . . . Down in the hole, lingeringly, the gravedigger puts on the forceps. We have time to grow old. The air is full of our cries. (*He listens.*) But habit is a great deadener.

Habit keeps us from going mad, keeps us, Beckett says in his book on Proust, from noticing much of anything; all we see is what we always see, signals to act as we have always acted. We give meaning to our world by our characters, read the world in our habitual way, a way that makes sense of it for us, that creates and recreates the same relationships between ourself and the world, ourself and others. Art, which is often thought to be an attack on our habits, is, like them, only another way of making sense of things. Most films are more skillfully constructed, better plotted, and more engaging than the purgatorial device Clair imagines, his movie of recurrence. The diversion produced by art, the way art gives life a plot, something for us to expect, the way it makes life more meaningful, is similar to the ways we might plot our own lives, construct projects, make life more meaningful. Art cheats us of boredom, of what might follow from boredom, some transforming knowledge.

4.   The question, for Nietzsche, is not how to get off of a circling world with its absolute absence of the Absolute, but how to wake up to the fact that we are on one, and how to bear it. For if we wake up to the fact, if we face the "greatest stress," if we stopped expecting something better, then perhaps we might, Nietzsche thought, make this a more nourishing world. The transformation would have to occur right now, for this very moment will recur. ("How well disposed would you have to become to yourself and to life to crave nothing more fervently than this ultimate confirmation eternal and seal?") Nietzsche's question is how to put an end to this world—this illusion—to close time, to shut up shop.

5.   This is not a world we can bear, so we live in hopes of a better world. Or perhaps, as Nietzsche teaches, this isn't a world we can bear because we live in hopes of better world.

Things are progressing, we think. Things will be better in the future than they are now. We have plans. The capitalists have plans and the revolutionaries have plans. Our real life is not here, but moves farther and farther into the future. Things will be better then or, if not, the world will end, and it will all be put right in the next world; we suffer now, but then we will be clothed in glory. The ending will arrive and the ending will make sense of this suffering (a sense of an ending helps us make sense). This whole business will come out all right in the end:

> Vladimir: We'll hang ourselves tomorrow.
> (*Pause.*) Unless Godot comes.
> Estragon: And if he comes?
> Vladimir: We'll be saved.

It is this hope for history, this goal toward which history is marching, that separates well-formed Critical Realist works from the works of decadant writers like Marcel Proust or Samuel Beckett. (Frank Kermode, in *The Sense of an Ending*, agrees that it is this end point that allows us to make time meaningful, to give it form: "we project ourselves—a small humble elect perhaps—past the End, so as to see the structure whole, a thing we cannot do from our spot of time in the middle.") We know that we don't suffer for nothing for God sees our sufferings, and will redeem them in the end. (It is indeed a holy moly movement.) Or the next invention, the next novelty—a nuclear reactor, a new work of a great artist, a new interpretive principle—will save us from shortages, from lovelessness, from boredom, from despair.

6.   But all we want really is to go on hoping: "I have discovered," Pascal wrote, "that all the unhappiness of men arises from one single fact, that they cannot stay quietly in their chamber.... But on further consideration when after finding the cause of all our ills, I have sought to discover the reason for it, I have found there is one very real reason, namely the natural poverty of our feeble and mortal condition, so miserable that nothing can comfort us when we think of it closely."

> Vladimir: All I know is that the hours are long, under these conditions, and constrain us to beguile them with proceedings which—how shall I say—which may at first sight seem reasonable, until they become a habit. You may say it is to prevent our reason from foundering. No doubt. But has it not long been straying in the night without end of the abyssal depths? That's what I sometimes wonder. You follow my reasoning?

So as not to think of his condition too closely man must divert himself. "Yet when we imagine a king attended with every pleasure he can feel, if he be without diversion, and be left to consider and reflect on what he is, this feeble happiness will not sustain him; he will necessarily fall into forebodings of dangers, of revolutions which may happen and finally of death . . . : so that if he be without what is called diversion he is unhappy, and the more unhappy than the least of his subjects who plays and diverts himself." So the king hunts; the king dances; or, as he is a king, he watches his servants do it for him:

> Pozzo: (*He jerks the rope. Lucky looks at him.*) . . . What do you prefer; Shall we have him dance, or sing, or recite, or think, or—
>
> Estragon: Perhaps he could dance first and think afterwards if it isn't too much to ask him.
>
> Pozzo: . . . Dance, misery!
> *Lucky puts down bag and basket, advances towards front, turns to Pozzo. Lucky dances. He stops.*
>
> Pozzo: He used to dance the farandole, the fling, the brawl, the jig, the fandango, and even the hornpipe. He capered. For joy. Now that's the best he can do. Do you know what he calls it?
>
> Estragon: The Scapegoat's Agony.
>
> Vladimir: The Hard Stool.
>
> Pozzo: The Net. He thinks he's entangled in a net.

To divert oneself is to want what one has not got, what one hopes for: "those who philosophize on the matter and think men unreasonable for spending a whole day in chasing a hare which they would not have bought, scarce know our nature. The hare in itself would not screen us from sight of death . . . ; but the chase which turns our attention away from these, does screen us." What we think we wish from our diversions is an end to our diversions, the fulfillment of our hopes, that we might have the thing which we have not got, that we plot for. "Men have a secret instinct which impels them to seek amusement and occupation abroad, and which arises from the sense of their constant unhappiness. They have another secret instinct, a remnant of the greatness of our original nature, which teaches them that happiness in reality consists only in rest and not in stir. And of these two contrary instincts, they form within themselves a confused idea which hides itself from their view in the depths of their soul, inciting them to rest through excitement, and always to fancy that the satisfaction which they have not will come to them, if by surmounting whatever difficulties confront them, they can thereby open the door to rest."

But perhaps those who philosophize on the matter are themselves chasing after a hare. Jacques Derrida's work "deconstructs" such metaphysical systems as Hegel's which are founded upon an Absolute moment (of origin and goal) in which we will at last confront our Being in complete self-presence, where we will rest; these deconstructions show that given the nature of language the systems are founded upon impossibilities. Their central terms are contradictions that will turn away from us as we approach them, receding at the moment that we try to grasp them. (It is of the nature of language, which is a system of differences, that it cannot express identity; it can only reveal the same, the absolute identity, as it is lost, in the moment that it becomes absent.) We accept such Absolutes because they allow us to avoid seeing that we ourselves create the meaningfulness of our world; that we are, in Pascal's words, "born to know the universe and to judge all causes." There is no moment that we are moving towards; we have set this particular hare in motion. Philosophy can go on forever; it is indeed the proper activity for kings, for kings most require diversion; and this diversion will never end.

Pozzo: Stop! (*Lucky stops.*) Back! (*Lucky moves back.*) Stop! (*Lucky stops.*) Turn! (*Lucky turns towards auditorium.*) Think!

Lucky: Given the existence as uttered forth in the public works of Puncher and Wattmann of a personal God quaquaquaqua with a white beard quaquaquaqua outside time without extension who from the heights of divine apathia divine athambia divine aphasia loves us dearly with some exceptions for reasons unknown but time will tell and

suffers like the divine Miranda with those who for reasons unknown
but time will tell are plunged in torment plunged in fire whose fire
flames if that continues and who can doubt it will fire the firmament
that is to say blast hell to heaven so blue still and calm so calm with
a calm which even though intermittent is better than nothing but
not so fast and considering what is more that as a result of the labors
left unfinished.

This diversion could go on forever; and in fact Lucky's
philosophizing continues for several more pages, continues even
when "All three throw themselves on Lucky who struggles and
shouts his text;" and ends only when Pozzo thinks to seize Lucky's
hat. That shuts him up. This speech is Beckett's deconstruction.
Roland Barthes says, "As for the derision of language, it is always
extremely partial; I know only one example which actually hits the
target, by which I mean makes us feel the vertigo of a wrecked system: Lucky's monologue in *Waiting for Godot.*"

The impossible resolution of our search would bring us rest
or Being. It is not a hare but rest itself that we chase in philosophy,
but fortunately we have insured that it is untrappable. The consolation of philosophy is that it lacks any consolation; we must kick such
props away, Pascal says, if we are able to confront the natural poverty of our "feeble and mortal condition." "In Pascal," Fredric Jameson
writes, "the real and desolate truth of existence is revealed only
through a thoroughgoing reduction of existence to the present
instant: reality becoming visible to us only on condition that we divest ourselves of the mirages or ontological diversions of both future
and past, only on condition that we come to terms with the emptiness of life in the present."

> Vladimir: We wait. We are bored. (*He throws up his hand.*) No, don't
> protest, we are bored to death, there's no denying it. Good. A diversion
> comes along and what do we do? We let it go to waste. Come, let's get
> to work! . . . In an instant all will vanish and we'll be alone once more,
> in the midst of nothingness!

If we did not have our games we would, Pascal says, have to
confront our dying. We would be, as Vladimir says—with the peculiar weight Beckett contrives to give to the most literal meanings—

"bored to death." So it is that when it appears that Godot might have arrived the two tramps are terrified, become grotesquely rigid:

> Estragon: I hear nothing.
> Vladimir: Hsst! . . . (*They listen huddled together.*) Nor I. (*Sighs of relief. They relax and separate.*)
> Estragon: You gave me a fright.
> Vladimir: I thought it was he.
> Estragon: Who?
> Vladimir: Godot.
> Estragon: Pah! The wind in the reeds.

The child is searching for something that it itself has hidden; if it were to find it the child would hide it again. But, of course, the fact of death, the wind in the reeds, cannot be truly repressed. The more we try to repress our death, the more it shapes our lives at each moment. Frantically we seek that rest, that remnant of our original greatness that has become an image of death. "One effect of the incapacity to accept separation, individuality, and death," Brown writes in *Life against Death*, "is to eroticize death—to activate a morbid wish to die, a wish to regress to the prenatal state before life and separation began, to the mother's womb. . . . The sexual organizations . . . appear to be constructed by anxiety, by the flight from death and the wish to die." Out of our repressed death we make time itself: "More generally according to Hegel, time is what man makes out of death . . . time is negativity, and negativity is extroverted death." We avoid that fusion of the instincts, of the pleasure principle and the nirvana principle that "would be the equilibrium or rest of life that is a full life . . . satisfied with itself and affirming itself rather than changing itself." We might, in Brown's conjecture, have a life then that was not continually in pursuit of that unobtainable rest (now another face of death, of death eroticized) but one that has given up the chase. "It is the flight from death that leaves mankind with the problem of what to do with its own innate biological dying, what to do with its own repressed death. Animals let death be a part of life, and use the death instinct to die: man aggressively builds immortal culture and makes history in order to fight death." The repression of one sort of recurrence (that which would occur at each instant) creates a structure of deferment in which our efforts create only another and unconscious circling back to the repressed.

So we prefer to go on hoping, chasing, deferring our death, and so deferring our life as well. We prefer our diversions: and the greatest of these diversions is hoping itself. In Beckett's vision we have so much hope that we are blinded by it, and stumble about harming ourselves. Krazy Kat hopes that someday Ignatz Mouse will love her (him); much ingenuity must be used in reinterpreting the meaning of the brick that conks her on the head. We are cursed, Beckett says, with "pernicious and incurable optimism," "the haze of our smug will to live."

7. Our hoping for the return of an object (for what we desire is always something lost) is a way (in Ernest Bloch's analysis) of keeping the self as it is and so not dying. This hoping is a kind of fetishism, in which the desired object has the magical effect of preserving us despite time. Bloch, to preserve for Marxism our capacity for hope, wished to separate hope from this fetishism. Fredric Jameson describes Bloch's analysis:

> Yet the . . . "filled emotions" [such as greed as opposed to hope—an "expectation affect"] project their wish into a psychic state which is properly unreal; they project what Bloch calls an "inauthentic future." For they ask for fulfillment in a world at all points identical to that of the present, save for the possibility of the particular object desired and presently lacking. Such effects are primitive or infantile to the degree that they amount to magical incantations, a conjuring up of the object in question just exactly as we long for it, at the same time that we hold the rest of the world, and our own desire, magically in suspension, arresting all change. . . . As though everything in the world were not interrelated . . . in the most astonishing and imperceptible fashion! As though the very changes in the world . . . did not run the risk . . . of transforming ourselves to the point where we no longer desired [the object]. Such emotions . . . imply a provincialism of the present into which we are plunged so utterly that we lose the very possibility of imagining a future which might be radically . . . *other;* their analysis also implies . . . a keeping faith with the open character of the future . . . which holds to the prospect of the absolutely unexpected as the only expectation: the certainty . . . of the concrete new in its unimaginable plenitude.

Bloch's analysis of filled emotions destroys the ground that his "hope" might walk on; or it reduces it to an image very close to despair. What is called the unimaginable plenitude of the new might as well be called its unimaginable or unacceptable poverty. In fact it can have no name at all, for that would be to project our desire (and so our continued self) on it. It does not matter what object or value (equality, or freedom, say) one prays for; unless one imagines oneself going under, it is here a fetishism, a way of avoiding death, of keeping the self as it is and the world still beneath one's feet. And one's going under cannot truly be imagined; who would imagine it? It is another case of trying to watch one's own funeral. In the end one must hope for nothing one can imagine; a space that the plenitude of the future might occupy, a space from which one's desires are necessarily absent. But how can one hope for what one cannot imagine? One hopes then simply that time might continue (as undoubtedly it will without one's hoping) and without projecting oneself forward into it (fetishizing the self) for the self too will be transformed by time; and to make oneself the desired object that one will have again in the future would be only another strategy to keep the world still; oneself will also be transformed as the world is transformed. Thus one hopes neither for an object nor for one's own presence; one hopes for nothing at all. Few revolutionaries have accepted this discipline.

8.   "The disease of Industrial man," Illich says in *Deschooling Society,* is "expectation" that "looks forward to satisfaction from a predictable process which will produce what we have a right to claim." This Promethean ethos, Illich writes, is destroying our world, destroying our ecology, destroying our capacity for joy and surprise, destroying our resourcefulness (wisdom too comes to us as a commodity, certified by degrees received). As opposed to expectation Illich places "hope." What Illich calls hope, a kind of going naked without institutional protection, without machinery, looks a great deal like suffering. (As in Pascal, life becomes "visible to us only on condition that we divest ourselves of the mirages or . . . diversions of both future and past, only on condition that we come to terms with the emptiness of life in the present.")

9. It is as if, if we are going to put an end to this world, this world that expects the next world, we must finally give up hope— "Abandon hope all ye who enter here"—as if to accept suffering is to take up residence in hell.

10. Beckett's impossible discipline is to refuse this world utterly and completely, to make, in Herbert Marcuse's phrase, the "great refusal." (But Marcuse is a dialectician; his refusal is the negative image of another, a better world.) The great refusal is a line from Dante, said of a man who refused to become Pope; for this Dante put him in hell.

11. Valery said, "One can say that all that we know, that is to say all that we have the power to do, has finally turned against what we are." But this is not to say that we must only refuse what we think is bad, for to refuse all that we are is to refuse also to imagine the continuance of what is good. It is silence: to refuse even to make distinctions, thus refusing all that we know, all expectations. It is not to be patient—or a patient—for there is nothing to be patient for. It is to stop waiting; there is nothing to wait for. There is *nothing* to wait for. R. D. Laing writes: "'There's nothing to be afraid of.' The ultimate reassurance and the ultimate terror."

12. As soon as you pray for *something,* Meister Eckhart preached, you turn God into a god, into a idol, into a creature in your own image, though one who can protect you. He is only apparently more powerful than you are, however, for really he is the servant of your desires. (God is a machine operated by prayers. Machines are gods operated by the sacrifice that we have made of labor.)

The other way Eckhart puts forward is that you might by silence open yourself to God, to his presence in you in the present, not your presence to yourself (or to his presents) but his birth in the most utterly hidden part of your soul. It is not something that intelligence can conceive. (The negative way: what you can conceive of is not God. One must eliminate one's conceptions, including one's conception of his inconceivability; and the conception of elimination.) What is God is death to you; and the death of the self is life to God. God is not your health, nor is he your sickness. (That is, this is not dialectics, nor simple reversal—the opposite image is not true contrary.) He is not your imaginations of your death, which you make up yourself and so are watching, but your actual death, which is unimaginable to you. To pray "his will be done," is, Simone Weil says, the only possible prayer; but it is not a prayer to him, but to help you suffer the world with a contrite heart. For his will is done; there is no need to pray, only to be silent.

13.   Getting rid of hope is harder than it looks. We are infinitely clever about hoping. If the body is defeated it is good for the soul. If the revolution is defeated it clears the way for further tactical progress. (The Marxist theoretician Régis Debray writes, "But the blood shed in Shanghai . . . must not be inscribed in the deficit column of the Revolution, as though it were the result of an error of judgement . . . the theoretical proof that an isolated urban insurrection cannot achieve victory in a semi-colonial country . . . had to be made in *practice*.") We're never lost because we can always learn from our mistakes.

14.   Getting rid of hope (which is to say, in Nietzsche's terms, killing god) should not be confused with eschatology, the hope of the end of the world (how long have we warmed ourselves on those flames!) or with Christianity, in which the son of God, our only hope, was utterly killed, only to be fully resurrected. In the last days things will finally make sense. (They won't.) They will have an order, an importance. (They won't.)

When the boy messenger comes for the second time in *Waiting for Godot,* he has forgotten the tramps' names, forgotten he ever saw them before. When the young child appears in *Endgame,* at the end, everyone has the good sense to ignore him.

15.   Giving up hope now in order to get something, a little something, back in the end—eternal life, say—is the oldest trick in the book. It was a fortunate fall; or as Bunyan said, it is good to be on the ground for then there is no farther to fall. But thinking it is good to fall, planning to take a fall, waiting to fall, practicing falling, lying there happy and full of hope, or dazed and full of hope, are all ways of cheating despair (our only hope). Another way is falling artistically, with a certain style and grace (and waiting for applause).

We have to put an end to artistic falling, to endgames, or our bad faith will undo us. In "The Aesthetics of Silence," Susan Sontag writes:

> Silence is a prophecy, one which the artist's actions can be understood as attempting both to fulfill and to reverse.
>
> As language points to its own transcendence in silence, silence points to its own transcendence—to a speech beyond silence.
>
> But can this whole enterprise become an act of bad faith if the artist knows *this*, too?

16. The revolutionary thinks he has an endgame, and perhaps the real revolutionary does. "The revolutionary," Nechayev said, "is a dead man." He is the spark, Lenin said, and when the prairie catches fire the spark—theoretically at least—is consumed, dies into the mass. The revolution is the end of the revolutionary; he is no longer recognizable to himself as he was; it is the end of his leadership, his role, his plan. Usually though, he has one more plan. Even Sorel, who was savage on how parliamentary revolutionaries (an impossible contradiction of terms, he thought) would never put an end to their own leadership, their plans, said, "The idea of technological continuity dominates the whole of the Marxian position." The myth of the general strike, the advent of socialism, is a total transformation for Sorel, a total conflagration. But something here is saved back from the fire. Instead of a fetishism of the commodity, there is a fetishism of the tools of production. And as we know from Bloch, to imagine a hoped for object is to imagine also a continuation of the self.

17. To Beckett, we are like the old people in *Acts*. We have always our one treasure, our ego, our one image, our project that we want to keep back from the flood, and so keep back ourselves.

But a certain man named Ananias, with Sapphira his wife, sold a possession.

And kept back part of the price, his wife also being privy to it, and brought a certain part, and laid it at the apostles' feet.

But Peter said, Ananias, why hath Satan filled thine heart to lie to the Holy Ghost, and to keep back part of the price of the land?

Whiles it remained, was it not thine own? and after it was sold, was it not in thine own power? why hast thou conceived this thing in thine heart? thou hast not lied unto men, but unto God.

And Ananias hearing these words fell down, and gave up the ghost: and great fear came on all them that heard these things.

[*Acts*, 5:1-5]

18.   To give up hope, to give up our plans, is a hard business. Beckett's works are a catalogue of all the ways there are for continuing to hope though you know you should end things; ways to keep from touching bottom, returning to earth, to keep from silence, from despair, from chaos. But all new information, the ecologist Gregory Bateson says, comes from chaos, from noise. New information comes from the unexpected, the unknown, the misinterpretation, the slip of the tongue, the mistake. Other than that there is only the already known, the planned, the expected. But the ego is capable of nearly infinite synthesizing. It makes even our mistakes therapeutic, fits them into the old order. ("People are wont to speak to the necessity of a new order of things," Durkheim writes. "Men in the grip of their personal ego, and of time adhering to it, can only give birth to an 'old' order. A new order is, correctly speaking, one which is renewed hourly.") An experience of chaos, of ground, is the hardest experience to have (let alone bear).

We keep from touching ground, from despair by telling stories. "All sorrows can be borne," Isaak Dinesen wrote, "if you put them into a story or tell a story about them." Beckett's old men are always telling stories. "I invented it all in the hope it would console me, help me to go on, allow me to think of myself as somewhere on the road, moving between a beginning and an end, gaining ground, losing ground, getting lost, but somehow, in the long run, making headway. All lies." Beckett's old men hear voices, repeat voices, put the voices into stories. (Silence like the absolute, is a goal that cannot be *mentioned*.) If they did not repeat these voices they would be crushed by them. Repeating them they create one more voice. And of course Beckett's old men are themselves stories.

We keep from despair by praying to God, not only that he might answer our prayers, but that he might be, as he was for Job, our audience, mute to our act. (He might understand, he might be shamed by it, might forgive us.)

> Estragon: Do you think God sees me?
> Vladimir: You must close your eyes.
> (*Estragon closes his eyes, staggers, worse.*)
> Estragon: (*stopping, brandishing his fists, at the top of his voice.*)
> God have pity on me!
> Vladimir: (*vexed*). And me?
> Estragon: On me! On me! Pity! On me!
> Enter Pozzo and Lucky. Pozzo is blind.
> *Lucky burdened as before.*

If we were to despair (it's our only hope) then our suffering must not mean anything. (It is impossible to utter a sound, to perform an act, to see an object that means nothing! All we can do is to signify meaninglessness, and by signifying it, defeat our purpose.) Our suffering is not a punishment from God, or a way to salvation; it isn't a trial or a test. There must be no audience: no superego, or watching agency.

> Estragon. Oh, yes, let's go far away from here.
> Vladimir. We can't.
> Estragon. Why not?
> Vladimir. We have to come back to-morrow.
> Estragon. What for?
> Vladimir. To wait for Godot.
> . . . .
> Estragon. And if we dropped him? (*Pause.*) If we dropped him?
> Vladimir. He'd punish us.

19. If there is no audience for our suffering, there is no drama, no tragedy, no one to watch the suffering (the audience for the tragedy and the god become one in the act of sacrifice that is the tragedy). There is no one to be terrified by it, no one to give or find atonement with. Beckett is an artist who looks forward yearningly (but his yearning is far too beautiful) to the end of audiences, the end of art. Stanley Cavell writes in his beautiful essay on *Endgame*:

> This ought to seem a set of goals split against itself: as though the end of the game will be to show that the game has no winner, the moral of the story to show there is no moral anyone can draw, its art directed to prove that art—the grouping of details to an overwhelming expression—does not exist; the games, plays, stories, morals, art— all the farcing of coherent civilization—come to nothing, are nothing. To accomplish this will seem—will be—the end of the world, of *our* world. . . . What used to seem life's leaven, the source of meaning and coherence, the shelters from chaos and destruction, have now grown to shut out existence; morality, art, religion, and the rest, lead lives of their own, grown out of hand, that shear man's existence from him. God shut us in. The result is that the earth is blotted out for man, sealed away by a universal flood of meaning and hope.

It is a difficult business to give up art. Beckett writing of the painter Bram Van Velde, speaks what is true of his own work. "He is the first to admit that to be an artist is to fail, that failure is his world, and to shrink from it art and craft, good housekeeping, desertion. I know that all that is required now to bring even this matter to an acceptable conclusion, is to make of this submission, this admission, this fidelity to failure, a new occasion . . . and of the act, which is unable to act, obliged to act, an expressive act, even if only of itself, of its impossibility, of its obligation."

The coherence of the performing self keeps reasserting itself. It is hard not to gesture meaningfully and difficult to fail. Or as Nietzsche said, "Man would rather take the void for his purpose than be void of purpose."

John Cage, I think, has come closest to failure that does not mourn, that is bracing by its lack of pathos; such pathos would signify a loss, would defeat the lack of purpose. In his silent compositions the audience makes the noises, performs the piece, if only it remains "undistracted," faithful to what it is doing, the poverty of the moment and what it provides; it is without diversion; and any preconceptions about art will deafen it to what is happening. In his chance compositions Cage has taken up with pleasure Mallarmé's negation; indeed a throw of the dice does not abolish chance. Cage shows his fidelity further by insisting that his chance compositions be performed exactly as they are notated. Perhaps through accepting chance one receives more abundantly; a new realism is obtained. Cage has said, "I imitate nature not in its appearances, but in its manner of operation." The world is returned to us as if for the first time, for matter after all is only large statistical aggregates of chance particles which are moving randomly. Chance and necessity (as in tragedy) are the same. Cage then does not succeed in failing entirely; he is a transitional figure; but at least here tragedy returns as farce.

20. "To think it won't all have been for nothing," Hamm cries out in *Endgame*, and the stage direction says his face is filled with anguish.

Beckett's teaching is that we have to accept that it is all for nothing, with not one particle held back. "Solitude, emptiness, nothingness, meaninglessness, silence," these Cavell writes, "are Beckett's goals."

21. Perhaps then if we give ourselves up hopelessly to silence there is some hope for us. (But not, Sontag warns, if we think so.)

In a letter to Marianne Moore, William Carlos Williams wrote of his despair, and the "inner security it brought him": "That security is something which occured once when I was twenty, a sudden resignation to existence, a despair if you wish to call it that —but a despair which made everything a unit, and at the same time a part of myself. I suppose it might be called a sort of nameless religious experience. I resigned, I gave up."

If it was a religious experience, it was, Williams reminds us, "nameless"—and not only because it was outside any church, but a religious experience without preconception, without hope. A dive into the muddy Passaic River is the metaphor Williams uses for it in his early poems. "A sudden resignation to existence"—that is the form our accommodation must take in this world without God. (It is not even a resignation: what are we resigning from? It is not an accommodation, for who is giving ground, being accommodating, and who being accommodated?) If we give ourselves up, Williams writes—give up those boundaries created by our purposeful plans for self-preservation—then it is all returned to us, all but our selves; the world becomes a part of ourselves, ourselves part of the world, an "interpenetration both ways." This is, J. Hillis Miller writes in *Poets of Reality*, the end of drama and art as we have known it, (for the lyric too assumes a plaint): "To give up the ego means to give up all those dramas of inter-change of subject and object, self and world, which have been central to Western philosophy and literature. The poet's resignation puts him beyond romanticism. After his resignation there is always and everywhere only one realm. Consciousness permeates the world and the world has entered the mind."

22.   By giving up our plans, the chatter of the ego, the attempts to preserve the self as it is, the object becomes empty. There is space then for the entry of the unconscious into the object. By this entry the object becomes an oracle, a symbol.

Symbolism is the silent discourse of the unconscious within the object. ("Say it!" Williams writes in *Paterson*, "no ideas but in things.") Silent because the unconscious is a silence to the ego; it is what Beckett calls the unnameable. It cannot ever be fully possessed by consciousness, made part of the ego, kept back from loss by being named. The object is always beyond reach, never to be attained, not to be hoped for, fetishized; it is lost. The silence cannot be translated into speech, only interpreted, commented on by words that might themselves become symbols.

The entry of the unconscious into the object makes the object part of our own body. There is nothing which is not part of us, nothing therefore on which we do not depend. And there is nothing else to depend on, having surrendered our hopes, surrendered finally to the world. (There was no one to accept the surrender, no ceremony to mark the last moment. For if there had been a ceremony we would have prolonged it endlessly; that is our art.) We have no prop to save us from our own body, from the immense importance of things: this table, this chair, this typewriter, numinous with a being that cannot be possessed, held back or held back from:

so much depends
upon

a red wheel
barrow

glazed with rain
water

beside the white
chickens.

GESTURING
WITH
MATERIALS

'NO IDEAS BUT IN THINGS'

Art is an anticipation of the way all work will be in the society of the future.

—SOREL, Reflections on Violence

Art for Herbert Marcuse is a world elsewhere, a world created by aesthetic form: "'Aesthetic form' means the total of qualities (harmony, rhythm, contrast) which makes an oeuvre a self-contained whole, with a structure and order of its own. . . . By virtue of these qualities the work of art *transforms* the order prevailing in reality. This transformation is 'illusion' but an illusion which gives the contents represented a meaning and a function different from what they have in the prevailing universe of discourse. Words, sounds, images from another dimension, 'bracket' and invalidate the right of the established reality" (81). Art transforms the order prevailing in reality, but not reality; it transforms that order only within the world elsewhere provided by form.

But as Marcuse knows, it is this very aspect of art, its self-contained quality, its being a world elsewhere, that has given the art of this century a bad conscience: "an aesthetic realm, self-sufficient, a world of aesthetic harmony which leaves the miserable reality to its own devices. It is precisely this 'inner truth' . . . which today appears as mentally and physically intolerable, false, as part of the commodity culture" (88).

Marcuse would like art to be less anxious about itself. (Compare, however, Picasso's remark, "What forces our interest is Cézanne's anxiety—that's Cézanne's lesson.") Art, Marcuse says, provides us with images of how things should (but never will) be. Art, by doing this—which it is able to do because of the transformation provided by aesthetic form—fulfills both its true nature and its political function at once. "Where the work no longer sustains the dialectical unity of what is and what can (and ought to) be, art has lost its truth, has lost itself. And precisely in the aesthetic form are this tension and critical negating, transcending qualities of bourgeois art—its anti-bourgeois qualities" (93). By virtue of the aesthetic form art can provide images which are a criticism of life.

Nonetheless, like a wilfully bad (or wilfully good) child, art refuses to be comforted. Duchamp, Artaud, American Action Painters like Jackson Pollock, Franz Kline, Willem de Kooning, composers like John Cage, are all in different ways protesting against aesthetic form. Artaud writes:

> everything that has not been born can still be brought to life if we are not satisfied to remain mere recording organisms.
> Furthermore when we speak the word "life" it must be understood we are not referring to life as we know it from its surface of fact, but to that fragile, fluctuating center which forms never reach. And if there is still one hellish, truly accursed thing in our time, it's our artistic dallying with forms, instead of being like victims burnt at the stake, signalling through the flames.

It is the artist, often, who is dissatisfied with form, sees in it restraint, constriction, the dead hand of the past. Artaud writes, "The actor does not make the same gestures twice, but he makes gestures, he moves, and although he brutalizes forms, nevertheless, behind them, and through their destruction, he rejoins that which outlives forms and produces their continuation."

Certain artists have felt themselves beating their heads against form, trying to destroy it, leave it behind, outrun it. The American Action Painters attempted to destroy, to subvert what we call "easel painting" by attacking in art the separateness of "formed" paintings.

"The easel painting," Clement Greenberg writes in *Art and Culture*, "the movable picture hung on the wall is a unique product of the West, with no real counterpart elsewhere. Its form is determined by its social function, which is precisely to hang on a wall. . . . The easel picture subordinates decorative to dramatic effect. It cuts the illusion of a box-like cavity into the wall behind it, and within this, as a unity, it organizes three dimensional semblances."

Action Painting in attacking this illusion attacked therefore the idea of the art work as a place we could escape into, a world elsewhere.

> From Giotto to Courbet, the painter's first task had been to hollow out an illusion of three dimensional space on a flat surface. One looked through this surface as through a proscenium into a stage. Modernism has rendered this stage shallower and shallower until now its backdrop has become the same as its curtain, which has now become all the painter has left to work on. . . .
>
> The picture has now become an entity belonging to the same order of space as our bodies; it is no longer the vehicle of an imagined equivalent of that order. Pictorial space has lost its inside and become all "outside." The spectator can no longer escape into it from the space in which he himself stands.

This art, Greenberg points out, is putting an end to "theater," an end to that special sacred space. "It is the kind of picture that dispenses with beginning middle and end. Though the all-over picture will hang on a wall, it comes very close to decoration—to the kind seen in wallpaper patterns that can be repeated indefinitely, and insofar as the 'all-over' picture remains an easel picture it infects the notion of the genre with a fatal ambiguity." "In using this convention as they do," Greenberg writes, "artists like Pollack are on their way to destroying it."

Brecht, too, wished to abolish the sacred space of the theater: the "alienation effect" would keep the audience from identifying with the characters:

> The spectator's need nowadays to be distracted from his daily warfare is continually reproduced by that daily warfare, but just as continually is in conflict with his need to control his own fate. Among such needs an artificial distinction is made between entertainment and maintenance; entertainment . . . is a continual threat to maintenance, since the spectator isn't led into the void—not into an unfamiliar world but into a distorted one—and he pays for his extravagances, which he regards as mere excursions, in real life. Identifying himself with his enemy does not leave him unmarked; it makes him an enemy to himself. Surrogates satisfy one's need and poison one's body.

No one could really act for the audience; they must make their fate themselves, outside the walls of the theater. The identification with the protagonist—which had been the basis of theater since the tragic sacrifice was first offered—would come to an end. Yet the Brechtian theater still leaves the spectator in a contemplative role—and that intentionally. He watches the play, no longer emotionally involved, in the detached spirit in which, Brecht imagines, spectators at some third-rate boxing match, lean back, smoke their cigars, consider the good and bad points of the fighters, as if weighing points in a philosophical argument. It is not that they are disinterested—the spectators remain proletarians—but that they are not, in watching the play, deceived by the emotional turmoil created by identification. The spectator, seeing his interests clearly, would go into the streets and complete in his life a process set in motion (or helped along) by viewing the play.

Walter Benjamin, in "The Artist as Producer," wishes to draw the interests of the audience, the workers, and the artist more closely together than even Brecht's model does. (For in Brecht's theater there is still a division between audience and actors.) This Benjamin does by considering the artists as workers; it is insofar as the artist reconsiders his work habits themselves, the way art is created, in line with his proletarian consciousness, considering himself not as divorced from the masses, but as producer (valuing, the Chinese Communists would say, "redness over technique") that he will be making a contribution to proletarian art. And there can be, of course, a similar movement from the other side of the proscenium: the artist as producer, the producer as artist. (I have stepped here outside of the bounds of Benjamin's essay.) In this way the "aura" that surrounds the work of art will be removed: on the grounds of spectator and artist meeting as producers (rather than as seer or philosopher presenting something made by mysterious processes to a public that must remain, because of that mystery, distant from it). After the end of "theater" as sacred space—the sacred space of politics, the theater of history, the theater of sacrifice—we find the unity of artist and worker as laborers. We could well say that any activity will become as privileged in its access to the sacred as any other.

This protest, in Artaud's writings in *The Theater and Its Double*, in Greenberg's description of Pollock's paintings, should I think have been taken more seriously by Marcuse. These artists wanted to put an end to illusion, to the distinction between the space of the painting and the space our bodies occupy, to the world elsewhere, the separate realm of the "art work."

In *The Tradition of the New*, Harold Rosenberg brings many of these themes together (indeed, it was he who was often their first interpreter):

> At a certain moment the canvas began to appear to one American painter after another as an arena in which to act—rather than as a space in which to reproduce, re-design, analyze or express an object, actual or imagined. What was to go on the canvas was not a picture but an event.
>
> The painter no longer approached the easel with an image in his mind; he went up to it with material in his hand to do something to that other piece of material in front of him. The image would be the result of this encounter.
>
> . . . .
>
> In gesturing with material the esthetic too has been subordinated. Form, color, composition, drawing, are auxiliaries, any one of which—or practically all, as has been attempted logically with unpainted canvases—can be dispensed with. What matters always is the revelation contained in the act.
>
> A painting that is an act is inseparable from the biography of the artist. The painting itself is a "moment" in the adulterated mixture of his life—whether the moment means the actual minutes taken up with spotting the canvas, or the entire duration of a lucid drama conducted in sign language. The act-painting is of the same metaphysical substance as the artist's existence. The new painting has broken down every distinction between art and life.

Marcuse's aesthetics do not, I think, take the artist's unhappiness at his own situation seriously enough, and so must dismiss much contemporary art as "non-art": "anti-forms which are constituted by the mere atomization and fragmentation of traditional forms; poems which are simply ordinary prose cut up into verse lines, painting which substitutes a merely technical arrangement of parts and pieces for any meaningful whole . . . But the anti-forms are incapable of bridging the gap between real life and art" (94).

But, as Rosenberg writes, "The critic who goes on judging in terms of schools, styles, form—as if the painter were still concerned with producing a certain kind of object (the work of art) instead of living on the canvas, is bound to seem a stranger."

Of course the artist *fails*. The art activity—living on the canvas—becomes an art work, hung in a museum. The canvas is "prized within the category of painting values and hangs on the wall," Rosenberg writes in *The Anxious Object:*

> in sum its being a work contradicts its being an action. . .
>
>   To the literal mind the presence of a contradiction invalidates either the description or the thing described. Yet it is precisely its contradiction, shared with other forms of action (since all action takes place in a context by which its purpose may be reversed) that makes Action Painting appropriate to the epoch of crisis.

Rilke called poetry the marks the dancer's hands made on the walls of his cell; and in a sense this means that the dancer-poet needs his cell for the tension that is the drama of his dance. The action painter needs the restriction of form—the sense of life that separates life from art—in order to have something to batter his head against. Schoenberg told Cage that if he couldn't learn harmony he would always be beating his head against a wall. Cage said "I'll beat my head against the wall until the wall falls down." The action painter is making a display of his condition; he needs the condition in order to have the resources to make the display. If his prison did not exist he might have to create one—or cease to be a "painter" in the sense that we know. We cannot expect "art" (as we presently think of it) to accomplish that cessation; and even—as I intend to argue—if we think of all our activities as art activities, we must still come to live that new way, must fully change our consciousness, in order to free the painter from his prison. It is towards this change of consciousness that the action painter's activity points. He is a *transitional* figure.

If the artist is dissatisfied with form, who is it that needs works of art?

Closed form is the art activity seen as object, and the object as an object of "aesthetic contemplation." "Perhaps," Marcuse writes, "this art presupposes on the part of the recipient that distance of reflection and contemplation, that self-chosen silence, and receptivity, which today's living art rejects. This non-behavioral, non-operational art . . . does not activate anything but reflection and remembrance" (102). The emotions aroused by art—moral, physical, sexual—are contained by form, "broken," "sublimated." The emotions become themselves further material for contemplation. So the philosopher needs formed art, "works" of art, to be the object of his contemplation.

But the autonomous work of art—autonomous because separate from any reality, bracketed from it by form—is strangely dependent on philosophy. First the art work—as the criticism of life—has become a kind of philosophy. Then it finds itself dependent on theory for all its mediations with the rest of experience. It is philosophy which translates art into the political realm, into political theory, into guidelines for action. It is theory also that sets limits on what can and cannot be translated into such action. Theory determines which images in art are more "real," part of the higher order, and which are merely ridiculous—affronts to the higher reality. (Reality is circumscribed and revealed by theory.) Theory is the place for the universal abstract description of which art provides what we might call "special case" examples. A still life is the general critique applied to a particular fruit. "There is no work of art," Marcuse writes, "where the universal does not show forth in the particular configurations, actions, sufferings. 'Show forth' in an immediate sensuous rather than 'symbolic' form: the individual embodies the universal: thus he becomes the harbinger of a universal truth which erupts in his unique fate and place" (87). But, as one learns from Marcuse's own critique of philosophy in the second part of *One Dimensional Man*, it is in the nature of the abstract to control the concrete example; the universal dominates and governs the particulars. What is shown in art (in its existential truth) is known already in a higher form, in theory. And contemplation—philosophy—is not changed by art, rather it gains new materials for itself to philosophize about, new objects, new realms to contemplate. Art does not make philosophy into a new activity—"Philosophy for the Greeks was a mode of action," Kierkegaard said, pointing towards one possible transformation or return.

It is theory, too, that translates art into the political realm, insofar as it can be translated (as well as setting the limits on that translation). The art image is the goal of the revolution; but political theory determines how that goal might be moved toward—it can never be reached. Political theory for Marcuse is rationality: "The basic structure and dynamic of society can never find sensuous, aesthetic expression; they are in Marxian theory the essence behind the appearance, which can only be attained through scientific analysis, and formulated only in the terms of such an analysis. The 'open form' cannot close the gap between scientific truth and its aesthetic appearance" (125). It is "scientific truth" that must translate art into the domain of political practice.

As the philosopher benefits from form, so too is it perhaps the philosopher that constructs it, that helps to turn the art activity into the art work, the object of contemplation. Jeffrey Mehlman writes:

> . . . it must not be forgotten that American new criticism found fast allies among the ego psychologists. Thirty years after Freud had declared the main thrust of his discovery to be that the ego is not master of its own house, Ernst Kris was reassuring the academy that "regression in the service of the ego" might solve a good measure of the humanists' problems. If there could be any index of the French distrust of the metaphorics of wholeness, integrity, and the entire imaginative complex epitomized by the "seamless web" it is J. Laplanche's suggestion that the ego, in its constitutional imperviousness to unconscious truth (i.e. the fact of primary process thinking) might be afflicted with a "synthesis compulsion."

It is the ego, as philosopher or critic, that gathers up the pieces of the art activity to form them into a unity, a wholeness, an integrity, a harmonious web. The synthesis compulsion of the ego "creates" the work to be contemplated by the philosopher. It is a seamless work, a closed form, because it would be the open places, the stumbling blocks, the slips of the tongue, the broken parts, the silence, that would call forth the participation of the spectator's own unconscious, that would make him active, an artist, a co-creator of a never finished activity. The art activity would be reborn in him. But as a smooth object of contemplation the art work does not call forth one's participation, it does not ask for fresh outpourings of spirit; it is closed, smooth, harmonious. One is protected from it; this is the critic's function (or our own, if we act as critic) in making form. The work formed by the critical function is not dependent on our participation, our perception, but it is there forever, objectively. "The authentic oeuvre," Marcuse writes, "has indeed a meaning which claims general validity, objectivity" (89).

Masterpieces, Artaud said in his call for an end to them, are art activities that have been thoroughly recouped by the ego, by the critic—that no longer require participation, that repel it. They are works ready for the museum, things that no longer make us anxious, or overcome our defenses; the work is dead; or "beautiful."

It is, Artaud thought, the art collector, the critic, the passive contemplative spectator who needs masterpieces. As Duchamp wrote: "Properly any masterpiece is called that by the spectator, as a last resort. It is the onlooker who makes the museum, who provides the elements of the museum. Is the museum the final form of comprehension?" Art as activity then becomes art work because of the nature of our peculiar social organization, by which activities are turned into commodities. Duchamp further writes, "African wooden spoons were nothing at the time they were made, they were simply functional; later they became beautiful things, 'works of art.'" Art works are what we make of the activity of the artists. "Everyone knows," Rosenberg writes, "that the label Modern Art no longer has any relation to the words that compose it. To be Modern Art . . . has nothing to do with either the period in which the thing was made, nor with the intention of the maker. It is something that someone has had the social power to designate as . . . relevant to our epoch."

Criticism, even when Critical Theory, is part of the soothing absorbing process by which art finds its way into the museum, by which art that wants to be, to remain, activity (and the need to make an *assertion* of this is what turns it into a drama, a *work*) becomes art work, however scandalous, and then becomes not even scandalous, but beautiful, a masterpiece. There is a sentence in Marcuse's essay on art in *Counterrevolution and Revolt*, which records this sad process. "In a sense the confrontation between closed and open form seems no longer an adequate expression of the problem: compared with today's anti-art, Brecht's open forms appear as traditional literature" (123).

Criticism helps us to absorb into the past, into art history, an activity that could speak to and move us toward the future. (Jacques

Putman remarks that to someone on the shore the gestures and screams of a drowning man may look very beautiful. But the man isn't trying to be beautiful; he is just drowning.) "As Thomas Hess argued," Rosenberg writes, "art history lies in wait for Action Painting at its beginning, its middle and its end (what lies in wait for art history?)."

The art activity does often at first seem alien, even ugly. And in our age its alien quality is, Rosenberg writes, its value. It extends our sensibility, gives us news, tells us something we are not familiar with, something—that because it may change us—we are not comfortable with. Critical Theory by assimilating the alien into the realm of theory, and then into the realm of "beauty" though it seems to preserve art, actually assimilates it—as much as any festival of the arts—into the realm of already known, already named alienation, of alienation contained within theory. And so Critical Theory destroys art's ugliness, its real strangeness, in the name of a known kind of strangeness, one that is mediated by theory. Marcuse writes, "The most uncompromising, most extreme indictment has found expression in a work which precisely because of its radicalism repels the political sphere: in the work of Samuel Beckett there is no hope that can be translated into political terms, the aesthetic form excludes all accommodation and leaves literature as literature. And as literature the work carries one single message: to make an end with things as they are" (116-17). But it is also true that some of the things Beckett wants to put an end to are aesthetic form, art, the world elsewhere, Critical Theory, philosophy. It is an entire universe of discourse that he wants to put an end to, an entire consciousness, and if he were successful he could not be appreciated by theory, could not, in fact, be appreciated—a gourmet-like connoisseurship of art would be impossible; Beckett would have annihilated theory. The rest would be silence. Perhaps from this silence there might be a further creation, a creation out of nothing, but it would have to be in a new language.

Art, according to Marcuse's aesthetics, should be beautiful. But perhaps, as Rosenberg says, if it is to be really useful, genuine, prophetic, *new,* art is not beautiful, but ugly, anxiety-provoking, terrifying. Harold Rosenberg writes,

Form predominates in a work after it has become familiar to us: when the surprise or shock has passed we prize it for its beauty. It is, however, in their disquieting phase—when their strangeness cause them to seem outside of art—that innovating paintings work to expand our consciousness and sensibility. Esthetic values are then in a state of being violated and disarranged (not of being furthered as appears to hindsight). . . . To value the new is to invite confusion and what confusion is good for is not yet sufficiently appreciated. . . . A full grasp of the new is accompanied by a species of terror, of the sort not unknown to research scientists, explorers, mystics, revolutionaries.

Art can be ugly, anxiety-provoking; it is then the unknown, the attack on the self, Artaud's theater of cruelty, Duchamp's clowning, the miraculous as described by Kierkegaard: "N. B. God can only show himself to man in miracles, i.e. as soon as he sees God he sees a miracle. But by himself he is incapable of seeing miracles, for the miracle is his own annihilation. The Jews expressed this pictorially by saying that to see God was death. It is truer to say that to see God, or see miracles, happens by virtue of the absurd, for reason must stand aside."

As reason must stand aside for the Modern here imagined, so must "taste." Art, like John Cage's music, asks us to move beyond taste, to move beyond our "self" and in this we can see how new art and revolution are the same, both are attacks on the bourgeois ego. As activities become "works" there is a rise in the importance of "taste." Walter Benjamin writes: "Taste develops with the definite preponderance of commodity production over any other kind of production. As a consequence of the manufacture of commodities for the market place people become less and less aware of the conditions of their production—not only of the social conditions but of the technical conditions as well."

So Duchamp writes of his work, "It was necessary to reduce my personal taste to zero." Or Rosenberg, "An action isn't a matter of taste."

Action Painting is not done according to taste, not created according to the "laws of beauty." How could it be, since the image is not known until already created, a surprise to the ego of the artist as much as to the critic? Marcuse writes as if the laws of beauty, of form, preceded any content: "Again it is the rhythm of the verse which renders possible prior to all specific content, the eruption of the unreal reality and its truth. 'The laws of beauty' form reality in order to make it transparent" (100). But nothing precedes the creative act in action painting. "To work from a sketch," Rosenberg writes, "arouses the suspicion that the artist still regards the canvas as a place where the mind records its contents rather than itself the 'mind' through which the painter thinks by changing a surface with paint. . . . The apples weren't brushed off the table in order to make room for perfect relations of space and color. They had to go so nothing would get in the way of the act of painting. In this gesturing with materials, the esthetic too has been subordinated. . . . What matters always is the revelation contained in the act."

What is already known—the laws of beauty—is part of art history, not art. Art history is the already known, the surface of the mind; it is a resistance to be struggled against. Rosenberg writes:

> Human action . . . is the common denominator that animates work, combat and sign language. . . . It embodies decisions in which one comes to recognize oneself . . . Action is . . . a means of probing, of going from stage to stage of discovery. If someone asks me a question my answer will come from the surface of my mind. But if I start to write the answer, or to paint it, or to act it out, the answer changes. What is being done provides the clue to another thought. The materials I use—words, paint, gesture—become the means for reaching new depths, for unveiling the unexpected.

The image, the action painters tell us, is discovered only in the constant gesturing that is the art activity. Jackson Pollock wrote, "When I am in my painting, I'm not aware of what I'm doing. It is only after a sort of get acquainted period that I see what I have been about. I have no fears about making changes, destroying the images, etc. because the painting has a life of its own. I try to let it come through." The Action Painter does not (in terms of the familiar uses of the mind) know what he is doing. "Socrates' examination of the poets," Cornford writes, "had convinced him that they worked not with conscious intelligence but from inspiration, like seers and oracle mongers, who do not understand the fine language that they use."

Art as an activity, an action, is not an image already known, even in the mind, created according to canons of taste already known. It is something not known until made, and, as in Vico, known by being made. It is a corporeal imagination. "In such fashion, the first men of the gentile nations, children of nascent mankind, created things according to their own ideas. But this creation was entirely different from that of God. For God in his purest intelligence knows things, and by knowing them, creates them; but they, in their robust ignorance, did it by virtue of a wholly corporeal imagination. And because it was quite corporeal, they did it with marvelous sublimity; a sublimity such and so great that it excessively perturbed the very persons who by imagining did the creating, for which they were called 'poets,' which is Greek for 'creators.'"

Creation is less like the activity of following an outline ("the laws of beauty") than like that activity, the life of the world, which follows the unpredictable unknown or open-ended laws of evolution. To know the laws of evolution we would have to see the whole process, for we do not evolve alone, but with all other things, subjects in their own right, who are our co-creators. In evolution all creatures make the world together not according to plan, but in unconscious cooperation. All creatures in this way make beautiful things: themselves, their own bodies. As Marcuse remarks, "Thus Kant attributes the beautiful in nature to nature's capacity to form itself in its freedom, in an aesthetically purposive way" (66–67). A purposeless purposiveness Kant calls it, which was also Keats' definition of poetry.

The world is beautiful, and it too is action painting, a constant gesturing in materials, whose only comment on itself is its own further gestures. And the image created is always a surprise, I suppose, to those of us already here. The next stage of evolution is both a catastrophe and a preservation; it might well look ugly to us.

The end of art is conceivable, Marcuse writes, "only if men are no longer capable of distinguishing between true and false, good and evil, beautiful and ugly, present and future" (121). But bees for example can make none of these distinctions, and yet create beauty. Marcuse's distinctions are not those of art, but of art criticism. (Bees, I suppose, do not have art criticism.) In art history there is rather a principle very much like natural selection—what is useful in the creation of new art (and often not what critics expect) is kept on.

Bees are, of course, the creatures that Marx contrasts with men: bees create but not according to plan; only man creates according to already made plans. (Marx says "imagination," but in context I believe he means plan.) But perhaps the right relation between plan and activity, at least in art, is not one where the activity is subordinate to the plan—"carried out according to plan." Rather, the diagram is itself art; and the art that follows is an interpretation or misinterpretation of that diagram, a comment on it, not a representation of it.

Art, then, is thinking in materials, not creating something already known, but action painting. It is done according to William Carlos Williams's motto: no ideas but in things, a gesturing in materials. It is in these terms that Williams contrasts himself with the thinker—the man whose thought precedes the poem:

> But who, if he chose, could not touch the bottom of thought? The poet does not, however, permit himself to go beyond the thought to be discovered in the context of that with which he is dealing: no ideas but in things. The poet thinks with his poem, in that lies his thought, and that in itself is the profundity. . . .
>
> Therefore the thinker tries to capture the poem for his purpose, using his "thought" as the net to put his thoughts into. Absurd. They are not profound enough to discover that by this they commit a philosophic solecism. They have jumped the track, slipped out of category; no matter what the thought or the value, the poem will be bad, to make a pigeon roar.

Action Painting, like Williams's poetry, looks forward to that time when every activity is part of what Artaud called "that primary physics from which Spirit has not disengaged itself"—the end of alienation. That time "when the objects and their names would melt into one" will, Marcuse writes, never come. There will always for him be a tension between object and name, between subject and object, people and nature, thought and action. He escapes idealism. But perhaps there is also, as in action painting, as in nature, as in Williams's motto, a time when words and things become one, when we discover ourselves in our activity, when we speak ourselves in and through things, when we gesture with materials. ("This notion," Marcuse writes, "is false and oppressive: it would mean the end of art" [107].)

Art then, the action painters teach us, is thinking in materials, not creating something already known, following a plan. And perhaps politics is too. In "Organizational Questions of Russian Social Democracy," Rosa Luxemburg writes:

> In all these cases (of mass action) in the beginning was "the act" . . . .The same phenomenon—the limited role of the conscious initiative of the party direction in the formation of tactics—can be seen in Germany and all other countries. In general, the tactical policy of Social democracy in its main lines is not "invented"; it is the product of a progressive series of great creative acts in the often rudimentary experiments of the class struggle. Here, too, the unconscious comes before the conscious, the logic of the objective historical process before the subjective logic of its bearers. The role of the Social Democratic leadership is therefore of an essentially conservative character. On the basis of the new experience it attempts to develop the newly won terrain of the struggle. . . . But this attempt reverses itself and becomes a bulwark against further great innovations on a wider scale.

Here the critic is to the activity of art as the party is to the masses, as the conscious is to the unconscious. Critic, party, and ego take this gesturing with materials, and make it into the stuff of theory. (They have a synthesis compulsion.) The theory—the laws of form, the laws of the class struggle—is prescriptive on the activity of the artist, or the activity of the masses. It is essentially conservative, and stands against the masses' next innovation, the next step in history; it is trying to stop art, stop history, stop the activity of the masses in old gestures.

One might ask then: Is the right discourse for politics philosophy or poetry? Is history the stuff of primary process thinking, of the unconscious becoming conscious in materials, as in dreams? Do we make history as philosophers or under the guidance of the philosopher kings, even if the king is not the party, but the individual philosopher, enthroned in his own house—the ego? Or do we make history as poets or action painters do, gesturing beyond ourselves? Are the agents of revolution philosophers following a known image, copying a sketch provided by the party, or do we, like action painters, create something never before seen?

Art can become a preserve, a world elsewhere, formed by the ego, guarded by critics who mediate for us, where to a limited extent we allow ourselves to dream (sort of). To dream into things, and to dream about them. But, as the gifted clown Marcel Duchamp reminded us with his urinal (or Andy Warhol with his soup cans), anything can become an object for dreaming.

Perhaps then anything can be an object for interpretation, an object for the regard we give art (suddenly seeing in soup cans certain formal qualities) because art itself is not really a special location, a world elsewhere, except insofar as the audience makes itself art critics, becomes complicit with the guards, and calls art a special realm. Art is, I think, our activity, even now. Nietzsche writes:

> Metaphysics, morality, religion, science—in this book these things merit consideration only as various forms of lies: with their help one can have *faith* in life. "Life ought to inspire confidence": the task thus imposed is tremendous. To solve it, man must be a liar by nature, he must be above all an *artist*. And he *is* one: metaphysics, religion, morality, science—all of them only products of his will to art—In those moments in which man was deceived, in which he duped himself, in which he believes in life: oh how enraptured he feels . . . And whenever man rejoices he is always the same in his rejoicing: he rejoices as an artist."

The world of commodity production is itself guided not by rationality but by primary process thinking; it too is a gesturing with materials. It is the production of symbols ("fetishes") and it is done under circumstances organized—as Sorel points out—by symbols, by myths.

We are artists now, these teachers say, but we are ignorant of what we do, we are unconscious, we conspire in turning our activities into commodities. And by separating off a realm for dreaming, of a however attenuated protest against commodity production, we preserve the illusion that another realm is free of artistry, lies, dreaming, is "rational." But it is—Duchamp or Freud teaches us—already a kind of poetry, though we must have the eyes to see this. So the question is will we have conscious or unconscious poetry? And what kind of society will allow us to be conscious poets, consciously gesturing with materials?

NOTES

INTRODUCTION:
ECCENTRIC PROPOSITIONS

P. 4   "The petit-bourgeois . . ."
Barthes, *Mythologies*, p. 151.

P. 5   "The basic structure and dynamic of society . . ."
Marcuse, *Counterrevolution and Revolt*, p. 125.

"The philosophers," Marx wrote . . .
Marx, *Early Writings*, p. 423.

P. 6   "The Learned Chorus . . ."
Brecht, "The Baden Learning Play,"
in Munk, *Brecht*, p. 197.

P. 7   "The fight against the bourgeois ideas . . ."
Hinton, *Turning Point in China*, p. 103.

P. 8   The quarrel between the poet and the philosopher . . .
Plato, *The Republic*, pp. 321–40.

The artist "gratifies that senseless part . . ."
Plato, *The Republic*, p. 337.

"But satisfactory means . . ."
Plato, *The Republic*, p. 334.

P. 9   "But what of the artist . . ."
Plato, *The Republic*, pp. 332–33.

"Art," Rilke wrote . . .
Brown, *Life against Death*, p. 66.

P. 11   "From politics to poetry . . ."
Brown, "Reply to Herbert Marcuse,"
in Marcuse, *Negations*, p. 24.

"'Life ought to inspire' . . ."
Nietzsche, *The Will to Power*, p. 451.

"When the problem of psychoanalysis . . ."
Brown, *Love's Body*, p. 109.

P. 12   If there were . . .
Nietzsche, *The Will to Power*, p. 36.

"Marxism has many truths . . ."
Wheelwright and McFarlane, *The Chinese Road to Socialism*, p. 234.

P. 13   "It seems that a number of analysts . . ."
Freud, *Standard Edition*, vol. 23, p. 249.

"a poem containing history . . ."
Kenner, *The Pound Era*, p. 360.

P. 14   "Inside the bus . . ."
Williams, *Paterson*, p. 9.

HISTORY IN THE REVOLUTIONARY MOMENT

P. 19   "The whole race is a poet . . ."
Stevens, *Collected Poems*, p. 355.

"The modern literature of Ireland . . ."
O'Brien, "Passion and Cunning," in *Triquarterly*,
no. 23/24 (Winter–Spring 1972), p. 150.

"Is there a nation-wide multiform . . ."
Miller, *Poets of Reality*, pp. 72-73.

P. 20   "These tours . . . and Irish songs and novels . . ."
Yeats, *Explorations*, p. 414.

"Now and in time to be . . ."
Yeats, *Collected Poems*, p. 179.

"Poets and painters and musicians . . ."
Miller, *Poets of Reality*, p. 72.

"Few historians," Conor Cruise O'Brien writes . . .
O'Brien, "Passion and Cunning," p. 150.

P. 21   "Beautiful lofty things . . ."
Yeats, *Collected Poems*, p. 301

"A heroic era . . ."
Mandelstam, "The Word and Culture," in *Selected Essays*, p. 52.

P. 22   "Apples, bread, potatoes . . ."
         Mandelstam, "The Word and Culture," p. 50.

         "as though some ballad-singer had sung it all."
         Yeats, *Collected Poems*, p. 317.

         "John Alphonsus Mulrennan . . ."
         Joyce, *A Portrait of the Artist as a Young Man*, pp. 251–52.

         "I go to encounter . . ."
         Joyce, *A Portrait of the Artist as a Young Man*, pp. 252–53.

P. 24   "I thought that all art . . ."
         Miller, *Poets of Reality*, p. 69.

         "It helps originality . . ."
         O'Brien, "Passion and Cunning," p. 198.

         "In a diary note . . ."
         Ellmann, *Yeats: The Man and the Masks*, p. 211.

P. 25   "The elegiac presents . . ."
         Frye, *The Anatomy of Criticism*, p. 36.

         "The nineteenth autumn has come upon me . . ."
         Yeats, *Collected Poems*, p. 129.

         "Cultic twalette," as Joyce called it . . .
         Miller, *Poets of Reality*, p. 75.

P. 26   "A spot whereon . . ."
         Yeats, *Collected Poems*, p. 239.

P. 27   "Italy, Poland, Germany . . ."
         O'Brien, "Passion and Cunning," p. 179.

         "Surely among a rich man's . . ."
         Yeats, *Collected Poems*, p. 198.

         "The aura we feel . . ."
         Donoghue, *Yeats*, pp. 70–71.

P. 28   "The dead living in their memories . . ."
         Donoghue, *Yeats,* p. 70–71

         "We are building up a nation . . ."
         Ellmann, *Yeats: The Man*, p. 112.

         "Yet I am certain . . ."
         Donoghue, *Yeats*, p. 78.

P. 29   "What matter that you understand no word . . ."
         Yeats, *Collected Poems*, pp. 283–84.

         "I desire a mysterious art . . ."
         Ellmann, *Yeats: The Man*, p. 214.

P. 30   "Aura," Benjamin writes . . .
        Jameson, *Marxism and Form*, p. 77.

        "Aura is . . . a mysterious wholeness . . ."
        Jameson, *Marxism and Form*, p. 78.

P. 31   "I have met them at close of day . . ."
        Yeats, *Collected Poems*, pp. 177–80.

P. 32   "The revolutionary . . ."
        Payne, *The Life and Death of Lenin*, p. 26.

P. 33   "Money is good . . ."
        Yeats, *Collected Poems,* p. 227.

        In an elegy, Northrop Frye says . . .
        Frye, *Anatomy of Criticism*, p. 296.

P. 34   "Persecution says he . . ."
        Joyce, *Ulysses*, p. 331.

P. 35   "And I belong . . ."
        Joyce, *Ulysses*, p. 332.

P. 36   "The soldier takes pride . . ."
        Yeats, *Collected Poems*, p. 278.

        "Those masterful images . . ."
        Yeats, *Collected Poems*, p. 336.

P. 37   "covering the world with mud."
        Forster, *Aspects of the Novel*, p. 121.

P. 38   "Love loves to love love . . ."
        Joyce, *Ulysses*, p. 333.

        that it "preserves within people . . ."
        Berger, *The Moment of Cubism*, p. 14.

P. 39   "And while she gazed . . ."
        Joyce, *Ulysses*, p. 357.

P. 40   "*The Mystery Man* . . ."
        Joyce, *Ulysses*, p. 376.

P. 41   "If Socrates leaves . . ."
        Joyce, *Ulysses*, p. 213.

        "In 'Circe' his nature prevents . . ."
        Goldberg, *Joyce*, p. 93.

P. 42   "The word is not the expression of a thing . . ."
        Marcuse, *Reason and Revolution*, p. xi.

P. 43   Marcuse writes . . .
        Marcuse, *Reason and Revolution*, p. x.

There is a similarity, Marcuse notes . . .
Marcuse, *Reason and Revolution*, pp. x–xi.

"Dante Alighieri, so utterly found himself . . ."
Yeats, *Collected Poems*, p. 158.

P. 44   "Has the philosophy . . ."
         Yeats, *Mythologies*, pp. 304–5.

P. 46   "Planned production . . . means . . ."
         McLuhan, *The Gutenberg Galaxy*, p. 276.

P. 47   "the absolute absence of the Absolute"
         Beckett, *Our Exagminations*, p. 22.

P. 48   "reduced by cross multiplications . . ."
         Joyce, *Ulysses*, p. 725.

P. 49   "He that has eyes to see . . ."
         Freud, in Brown, *Love's Body*, p. 256.

         "I am quite content . . ."
         Atherton, *The Books at the Wake*, p. 169.

P. 50   Mythical thought "works by analogies . . ."
         Lévi-Strauss, *The Savage Mind*, pp. 20–21.

         As opposed to the mythological bricoleur . . .
         Lévi-Strauss, *The Savage Mind*, pp. 19–20.

P. 51   "If one calls bricolage the necessity of . . ."
         Derrida, in Macksey and Donato, eds., *The Language of Criticism and the Sciences of Man*, pp. 255–56.

         "Really it is not I who am writing . . ."
         Brown, *Closing Time*, p. 109.

P. 52   Yeats "thought he perceived in Joyce . . ."
         Ellmann, *The Identity of Yeats*, p. 187.

         "The man who can easily wed the crowd . . ."
         Baudelaire, *Twenty Prose Poems*, pp. 28–29

P. 53   "While he could 'do anything with language' . . ."
         Atherton, *The Books at the Wake*, p. 15.

P. 54   "get on top of each other . . ."
         Brown, *Closing Time*, preface.

P. 55   "According to Rilke . . ."
         Ellmann, *The Identity of Yeats*, p. 213.

         "All images can be dissolved . . ."
         Ellmann, *The Identity of Yeats*, p. 214.

P. 56   'But by writing . . ."
         Joyce, *Finnegans Wake*, p. 114.

P. 57   "It is not about something . . ."
         Atherton, *The Books at the Wake*, pp. 15–16.

         "A heroic era . . ."
         Mandelstam, "The Word and Culture," p. 52.

HISTORY AS THEATER; OR, TERROR AND SACRIFICE

All citations from *Hamlet* are from the Signet edition,
edited by Edward Hubler.

P. 61   "One is told that the Russians . . ."
         Empson, *Some Versions of Pastoral*, p. 5.

P. 64   "Each of these great historical tragedies . . ."
         Kott, *Shakespeare Our Contemporary*, pp. 6–7.

         "In 1789 . . ."
         Tolstoy, *War and Peace*, p. 1,314.

         "Killykill-killy."
         Joyce, *Finnegans Wake*, p. 4.

P. 66   "the king lets slip a sentence . . ."
         Kott, *Shakespeare*, p. 16.

P. 70   "Let be be finale of seem."
         Stevens, *Collected Poems*, p. 64.

P. 71   "In order to know . . ."
         Debray, *Revolution in the Revolution?*, p. 125.

         "He that has eyes to see . . ."
         Freud, in Brown, *Love's Body*, p. 256.

P. 73   "History had been 'unleashed.' . . ."
         Kott, *The Eating of the Gods*, p. 229.

         "When Dr. Lunde . . ."
         West, *Sacrifice unto Me*, pp. 146, 156, 157, 159.

P. 74   "confusion / Basis of renewals . . ."
         Pound, *The Cantos*, p. 92.

P. 75   "the absolute liquefaction . . ."
         Kojève, *Introduction to the Reading of Hegel*, pp. 21–22.

         "a pre-emptive counter-revolution . . ."
         Marcuse, *Counterrevolution and Revolt*, p. 1.

"Stripped to its essentials . . ."
Walter, *Terror and Resistance*, p. 9.

P. 77   "The revolutionary is a doomed man."
Nechayev, in Payne, *The Life and Death of Lenin*, p. 24.

"men come to believe . . ."
Unger, *Knowledge and Politics*, p. 75.

"Not being able to make what was just strong . . ."
Pascal, *Pensées*, p. 91.

P. 78   Brown's revision of Freudian theory . . .
Brown, *Life against Death*, pp. 167, 270.

"the rest of the body . . ."
Brown, *Love's Body*, p. 132.

P. 79   "This piece of instinctual satisfaction . . ."
Freud, *Standard Edition*, vol. 9, p. 187.

"Cosmos has become chaos again . . ."
Kott, *The Eating of the Gods*, p. 200.

P. 80   "In the first row of seats . . ."
Kott, *The Eating of the Gods*, pp. 227-28.

"The ritual . . . has turned . . ."
Kott, *The Eating of the Gods*, p. 207.

"a mystic union . . ."
Séjourne, *Burning Water*, p. 27.

P. 81   "a low witchcraft . . ."
Séjourne, *Burning Water*, p. 28.

"The adult ego . . ."
Freud, *Standard Edition*, vol. 23, pp. 237-38.

P. 82   "Christ," Pascal wrote . . .
Kott, *The Eating of the Gods*, p. 208.

When Bakhunin tried to imagine . . .
Cf. Joll, "The Revolution that Never Was," *Partisan Review*,
42, no. 1 (1975): 114-15.

P. 83   The revolutionary, Che Cuevara wrote . . .
Guevara, "Man and Socialism in Cuba," in *Venceremos!*, p. 399.

"Ch'en was becoming aware . . ."
Malraux, *Man's Fate*, p. 10.

"The ego . . . takes revenge . . ."
Luxemburg, *Selected Political Writings*, pp. 305-6.

P. 84   "It is the theory of . . ."
          Naipul, "India: New Claim on the Land," *New York Review of Books*,
          24 June 1976, p. 24.

          "Few people . . ."
          Friedenberg, *R. D. Laing*, p. 67.

          "Socialism," Sorel remarks . . .
          Sorel, *Reflections on Violence*, p. 151.

P. 85   "Man does not become man . . ."
          Brecht, "Against Lukacs," *New Left Review* 84 (March–April 1974): 40.

          "There were millions . . ."
          Malraux, *Man's Fate*, p. 13.

          "if by chance . . ."
          Sorel, *Reflections*, p. 121.

P. 87   "the tempestuous loveliness of terror . . ."
          Praz, *The Romantic Agony*, p. 26.

P. 88   "Beauty's nothing but . . ."
          Rilke, *Duino Elegies*, p. 21.

          "Dread," Kierkegaard wrote . . ."
          Kierkegaard, *Journals*, p. 79.

          "Pentheus is defenseless . . ."
          Kott, *The Eating of the Gods*, pp. 226–27.

P. 90   "a child is being beaten."
          Freud, *Standard Edition*, vol. 17, p. 177.

          "the pure culture of the death instinct . . ."
          Freud, *Standard Edition*, vol. 19, p. 53.

P. 91   "We are apt to think . . ."
          Freud, *Standard Edition*, vol. 20, p. 42.

P. 92   "At this stage . . ."
          Sartre, "Preface," Fanon, *The Wretched of the Earth*, p. 16.

"BURNING THE CHRISTMAS GREENS"; OR, DESPAIR

P. 97   Stubb, eyeing the wreck exclaimed . . .
          Melville, *Moby-Dick*, p. 545.

          "At the thick of the dark . . ."
          Williams, *Collected Later Poems*, p. 16.

P. 98   "Fire burns; that is the first law . . ."
         Williams, *Paterson*, p. 113.

P. 99   "The language, the language . . ."
         Williams, *Paterson*, p. 11.

         "It is difficult . . ."
         Williams, *Pictures from Breughel*, pp. 161–62.

         "Of which we drink . . ."
         Williams, *Paterson*, p. 117.

P. 100   "*BECAUSE IT IS SILENT*. . ."
         Williams, *Paterson*, p. 122.

         "The mind is the cause of our distresses . . ."
         Williams, *Pictures from Breughel*, pp. 75–76.

         "He would have the poem be . . ."
         Miller, ed., *William Carlos Williams*, pp. 100–101.

P. 101   "If you put God outside . . ."
         Bateson, *Steps to an Ecology of Mind*, pp. 367–68.

P. 102   "Why even speak of 'I' . . ."
         Williams, *Paterson*, p. 19.

         "Inseparable from the fire . . ."
         Williams, *Pictures from Breughel*, p. 178.

P. 105   "To shut up shop, dappy" . . .
         Joyce, *Finnegans Wake*, p. 23.

         "commodious vicus of recirculation."
         Joyce, *Finnegans Wake*, p. 3.

         "In what sense, then is Mr. Joyce's work . . ."
         Beckett, *Our Exagminations*, p. 22.

P. 106   "*The greatest stress* . . . "
         Kaufmann, *The Portable Nietzsche*, pp. 101–2.

         "The patients were described as 'cut off' . . ."
         Alvarez, *Beckett*, pp. 29–30.

         René Clair said . . .
         Cavell, *Must We Mean What We Say*, p. 119.

         "Vladimir: . . . Down in the hole . . . "
         Beckett, *Waiting for Godot*, p. 58.

P. 108   "Vladimir: We'll hang ourselves tomorrow . . ."
         Beckett, *Waiting for Godot*, p. 60.

         "we project ourselves . . ."
         Kermode, *The Sense of an Ending*, p. 8.

"I have discovered . . ."
Pascal, *Pensées*, p. 43.

"Vladimir: All I know is . . ."
Beckett, *Waiting for Godot*, p. 51.

P. 109   "Yet when we imagine a king . . ."
Pascal, *Pensées*, p. 44.

"Pozzo: . . . What do you prefer . . ."
Beckett, *Waiting for Godot*, pp. 26–28.

"those who philosophize . . ."
Pascal, *Pensées*, p. 44.

"Men have a secret instinct . . ."
Pascal, *Pensées*, p. 45.

P. 110   "born to know the universe . . ."
Pascal, *Pensées*, p. 47.

"Pozzo: Stop . . ."
Beckett, *Waiting for Godot*, p. 28.

P. 111   "As for the derision of language . . ."
Barthes, *Critical Essays*, p. 275.

"In Pascal, " Fredric Jameson writes . . .
Jameson, *Marxism and Form*, p. 139.

"Vladimir: We wait . . ."
Beckett, *Waiting for Godot*, p. 52.

P. 112   "Estragon: I hear nothing . . ."
Beckett, *Waiting for Godot*, p. 13.

"One effect of the incapacity . . ."
Brown, *Life against Death*, p. 115.

"More generally according to Hegel . . ."
Brown, *Life against Death*, p. 102.

"would be the equilibrium or rest of life . . ."
Brown, *Life against Death*, p. 90.

"It is the flight from death . . ."
Brown, *Life against Death*, p. 101.

P. 113   "pernicious and incurable optimism . . ."
Alvarez, *Beckett*, p. 14.

"Yet the . . . 'filled emotions' . . ."
Jameson, *Marxism and Form*, p. 126–27.

P. 114   "The disease of Industrial man . . ."
Illich, *Deschooling Society*, p. 152.

P. 115 "One can say that all that we know . . ."
Arendt, *On Violence*, pp. 86–87.

"'There's nothing to be afraid of.' . . ."
Laing, *The Politics of Experience*, pp. 37–38.

P. 116 To pray, "his will be done," . . .
Weil, *Waiting for God*, p. 218.

"But the blood shed in Shanghai . . ."
Debray, *Strategy for Revolution*, p. 135.

P. 117 "Silence is a prophecy . . ."
Sontag, *Styles of Radical Will*, p. 18.

"The idea of technological continuity . . ."
Sorel, *Reflections on Violence*, p. 150.

P. 118 "People are wont to speak . . ."
Brown, *Love's Body*, p. 235.

"I invented it all in the hope it would . . ."
Alvarez, *Beckett*, pp. 43–44.

P. 119 "Estragon: Do you think God sees . . ."
Beckett, *Waiting for Godot*, p. 49.

"Estragon: Oh, yes, let's go far away . . ."
Beckett, *Waiting for Godot*, p. 59.

P. 120 "This ought to seem a set of goals . . ."
Cavell, *Must We Mean What We Say*, pp. 148–49.

"He is the first to admit . . ."
Beckett, *Bram Van Velde*, p. 13.

"Man would rather . . ."
Cavell, *Must We Mean What We Say*, p. 150.

P. 121 "To think it won't all have been for nothing . . ."
Cavell, *Must We Mean What We Say*, p. 149.

"Solitude, emptiness . . ."
Cavell, *Must We Mean What We Say*, p. 156.

In a letter to Marianne Moore . . .
Miller, *Poets of Reality*, p. 287.

P. 122 "To give up the ego . . ."
Miller, *Poets of Reality*, p. 287.

P. 124 "so much depends . . ."
Williams, *Collected Earlier Poems*, p. 277.

GESTURING WITH MATERIALS

All citations in parentheses are pages numbers in Marcuse,
Counterrevolution and Revolt.

P. 127   "What forces our interest . . ."
Rosenberg, *The Anxious Object,* p. 188.

P. 128   "everything that has not been born . . ."
Artaud, *The Theater and Its Double,* p. 166.

"The actor does not make . . ."
Artaud, *The Theater and Its Double,* p. 12.

"The easel painting . . ."
Greenberg, *Art and Culture,* p. 154.

P. 129   "From Giotto to Courbet . . ."
Greenberg, *Art and Culture,* pp. 136–37.

"In using this convention as they do . . ."
Greenberg, *Art and Culture,* p. 157.

"The spectator's need nowadays . . ."
Brecht, *The Messingkauf Dialogues,* p. 103.

P. 131   "At a certain moment . . ."
Rosenberg, *The Tradition of the New,* p. 25.

"The critic who goes on judging . . ."
Rosenberg, *The Tradition of the New,* p. 28.

P. 132   "in sum its being a work . . ."
Rosenberg, *The Anxious Object,* p. 43.

P. 133   'Philosophy for the Greeks . . ."
Rosenberg, *The Anxious Object,* p. 37.

P. 134   " . . . it must not be forgotten . . ."
Mehlman, *Yale French Studies,* no. 48 (1972), p. 20.

P. 135   "Properly any masterpiece . . ."
Cabanne, *Dialogues with Duchamp,* p. 70.

"Everyone knows . . ."
Rosenberg, *The Anxious Object,* p. 36.

Jacques Putnam remarks . . .
Beckett, *Bram Van Velde,* p. 32.

P. 136   "As Thomas Hess argued . . ."
Rosenberg, *The Anxious Object,* p. 43.

P. 137   "Form predominates in a work . . ."
          Rosenberg, *The Anxious Object*, p. 189.

          "N. B. God can only show himself to man in . . ."
          Kierkegaard, *Journals*, p. 91.

          "Taste develops . . ."
          Benjamin, *Charles Baudelaire*, pp. 104–5.

          "It was necessary to reduce . . ."
          Cabanne, *Dialogues with Duchamp*, p. 48.

          "An action isn't a matter of taste."
          Rosenberg, *The Tradition of the New*, p. 38.

P. 138   "To work from a sketch . . ."
          Rosenberg, *The Tradition of the New,* p. 26.

          "Human action . . . is the common . . ."
          Rosenberg, *Artworks and Packages*, p. 222.

          Jackson Pollock wrote, "When I am in . . ."
          O'Hara, *Jackson Pollock*, p. 32.

          "Socrates' examination of the poets . . ."
          Plato, *The Republic*, p. 323.

P. 139   "In such fashion, the first men . . ."
          Vico, *The New Science*, p. xlvii.

P. 140   "But who, if he chose . . ."
          Williams, *Paterson*, "Author's Note" (unpaged).

P. 141   "In all these cases . . ."
          Luxemburg, *Selected Political Writings,* pp. 293–94.

          "Metaphysics, morality, religion . . ."
          Nietzsche, *The Will to Power*, pp. 451–52.

SELECTED
BIBLIOGRAPHY

Ali, Tariq. *The New Revolutionaries*. New York: W. Morrow, 1969.

Allan, D. M., ed. *New American Poetry*. New York: Grove Press, 1960.

Alvarez, A. *Samuel Beckett*. New York: Viking Press, 1973.

Arendt, Hannah. *On Violence*. New York: Harcourt, Brace & World, 1970.

Artaud, Antonin. *The Theater and Its Double*. New York: Grove Press, 1958.

Atherton, James S. *The Books at the Wake*. New York: Viking Press, 1960.

Barfield, Owen. *Saving the Appearances*. New York: Harcourt, Brace & World, 1965.

Barthes, Roland. *Critical Essays*. Translated by Richard Howard. Evanston: Northwestern University Press, 1972.

——. *Mythologies*. Translated by Annette Lavers. New York: Hill & Wang, 1972.

Bateson, Gregory. *Steps to an Ecology of Mind*. San Francisco: Chandler Publishing Co., 1972.

Baudelaire, Charles. *Twenty Prose Poems*. London: Jonathan Cape, 1968.

Beckett, Samuel. *Endgame*. New York: Grove Press, 1958.

——. *Happy Days*. New York: Grove Press, 1961.

——. *Three Novels: Molloy, Malone Dies, The Unnamable*. New York: Grove Press, 1958.

——. *Waiting for Godot*. New York: Grove Press, 1954.

Beckett, Samuel; Duthuit, Georges; and Putnam, Jacques. *Bram Van Velde*. New York: Grove Press, 1958.

Beckett, Samuel, et al. *Our Exagmination Round His Factification for Incamination of Work in Progress*. New York: New Directions Books, 1961.

Benjamin, Walter. *Charles Baudelaire*. Translated by Harry Zohn. London: New Left Books, 1973.

——. *Understanding Brecht*. Translated by Anna Bostock. London: New Left Books, 1973.

Berger, John. *The Moment of Cubism*. New York: Pantheon, 1969.

Bloom, Harold. *The Anxiety of Influence*. New York: Oxford University Press, 1973.

——. *A Map of Misreading.* New York: Oxford University Press, 1975.

Brecht, Bertolt. "Against Georg Lukács." In *New Left Review,* no. 84 (March-April 1974).

——. *The Messingkauf Dialogues.* Translated by John Willett. London: Methuen, 1965.

Brown, Norman O. *Closing Time.* New York: Random House, 1973.

——. "Daphne, or Metamorphosis." In *Myths, Dreams, and Religion,* edited by Joseph Campbell. New York: E. P. Dutton, 1970.

——. *Life against Death.* Middletown, Conn.: Wesleyan University Press, 1959.

——. *Love's Body.* New York: Random House, 1966.

——. "Metamorphoses II: Actaeon." In *American Poetry Review,* November-December 1972, p. 38.

Bugliosi, Vincent, with Gentry, Curt. *Helter Skelter.* New York: Bantam, 1974.

Cabanne, Pierre. *Dialogues with Marcel Duchamp.* Translated by Ron Padgett. New York: Viking Press, 1971.

Cage, John M. *Silence.* Cambridge, Mass.: M.I.T. Press, 1961.

——. *Writings, '67-'72.* Middletown, Conn.

——. *A Year from Monday.* Middletown, Conn.: Wesleyan University Press, 1967.

Campbell, Joseph, ed. *Myths, Dreams, and Religion.* New York: E. P. Dutton, 1970.

Cavell, Stanley. *Must We Mean What We Say?* New York: Charles Scribner's Sons, 1969.

Debray, Régis. *Revolution in the Revolution?* Translated by Bobbye Ortiz. New York: Grove Press, 1967.

——. *Strategy For Revolution.* Edited by Robin Blackburn. New York: Monthly Review Press, 1970.

Derrida, Jacques. *Speech and Phenomena and Other Essays on Husserl's Theory of Signs.* Translated and introduction by David B. Allison. Evanston: Northwestern University Press, 1973.

——. "White Metaphor." In *New Literary History,* 6, no. 1 (Autumn 1974).

Donoghue, Denis. *William Butler Yeats.* New York: Viking, 1971.

Eagleton, Terry. *Criticism and Ideology.* London: New Left Books, 1976.

Ellmann. Richard. *The Identity of Yeats.* New York: Oxford University Press, 1964.

——. *James Joyce.* New York: Oxford University Press, 1959.

——. *Yeats: The Man and the Masks.* New York: E. P. Dutton, 1948.

Emerson, Ralph Waldo. *Selected Essays, Lectures, and Poems.* New York: Washington Square Press, 1965.

Empson, William. *Some Versions of Pastoral.* New York: New Directions Books, 1960.

Engles, Frederick. *The Origin of the Family, Private Property and the State.* Edited by Eleanor Burke Leacock. New York: International Publishers, 1970.

Erikson, Erik H., ed. *The Challenge of Youth.* Garden City, N.Y.: Anchor Doubleday, 1963.

Fanon, Frantz. *The Wretched of the Earth.* Translated by Constance Farrington. New York: Grove Press, 1966.

Forster, E. M. *Aspects of the Novel.* New York: Harcourt, Brace & World, 1954.

Freud, Sigmund. *The Standard Edition of the Complete Psychological Works.*

Translated by James Strachey. London: The Hogarth Press and the Institute of Psycho-Analysis, 1963.

Friedenberg, Edgar Z. *R. D. Laing.* New York: Viking, 1973.

Frye, Northrop. *Anatomy of Criticism.* Princeton: Princeton University Press, 1971.

Gendzier, Irene L. *Frantz Fanon.* New York: Vintage, 1974.

Goldberg, S. L. *Joyce.* New York: Capricorn Books, 1962.

Greenberg, Clement. *Art and Culture.* Boston: Beacon Press, 1961.

Guevara, Ernesto Che. *Venceremos!* Edited by John Gerassi. New York: Simon & Schuster, 1968.

Heidegger, Martin. *Existence and Being.* Chicago: Henry Regnery Co., 1949.

———. *Identity and Difference.* Translated by Joan Stambough. New York: Harper & Row, 1969.

Heisenberg, Werner. *Physics and Beyond.* Translated by Arnold J. Pomerans. New York: Harper & Row, 1971.

Herriman, George. *Krazy Kat.* New York: Grosset & Dunlap, 1969.

Hinton, William. *Turning Point in China.* New York: Monthly Review Press, 1972.

Hirschman, Jack, ed. *Antonin Artaud Anthology.* San Francisco: City Lights Books, 1965.

Illich, Ivan. *Deschooling Society.* New York: Harrow Books, Harper & Row, 1972.

———. *Tools for Conviviality.* Edited by Ruth Nanda Anshen. New York: Harper & Row, 1973.

Jameson, Fredric. *Marxism and Form.* Princeton: Princeton University Press, 1971.

Joyce, James. *Finnegans Wake.* New York: Viking, 1939.

———. *A Portrait of the Artist as a Young Man.* New York: Viking Press, 1964.

———. *Ulysses.* New York: Modern Library, 1946.

Kenner, Hugh. *The Pound Era.* Berkeley and Los Angeles: University of California Press, 1971.

Kermode, Frank. *The Sense of an Ending.* New York: Oxford University Press, 1967.

Kierkegaard, Søren. *The Concept of Dread.* Translated by Walter Lowrie. Princeton: Princeton University Press, 1957.

———. *The Journals of Kierkegaard.* Edited by Alexander Dru. New York: Harper & Row, 1959.

Kojève, Alexandre. *Introduction to the Reading of Hegel.* Edited by Allen Bloom. Translated by James H. Nichols, Jr. New York: Basic Books, 1969.

Kott, Jan. *The Eating of the Gods.* New York: Random House, 1973.

———. *Shakespeare Our Contemporary.* Translated by Boleslaw Taborski. Garden City, N.Y.: Doubleday Anchor, 1966.

Laing, R. D. *The Politics of Experience.* New York: Ballantine Books, 1967.

Lenin, V. I. *The State and Revolution.* Peking: Foreign Languages Press, 1965.

———. *What Is to Be Done?* New York: International Publishers, 1969.

Lévi-Strauss, Claude. *The Savage Mind.* Chicago: University of Chicago Press, 1966.

Lukács, Georg. *Lenin.* Cambridge, Mass.: M.I.T. Press, 1970.

Luxemburg, Rosa. *Selected Political Writings.* New York: Monthly Review Press, 1971.

Macheray, Pierre. *A Theory of Literary Production.* London: Routledge & Kegan Paul, 1978.

Macksey, Richard, and Danato, Eugenio, eds. *The Languages of Criticism and the Sciences of Man: The Structuralist Controversy.* Baltimore: The Johns Hopkins Press, 1970.

McLuhan, Marshall. *The Gutenberg Galaxy.* Toronto: University of Toronto Press, 1962.

Malraux, André. *Man's Fate.* Translated by Haakon M. Chevalier. New York: Modern Library, 1961.

Mandelstam, Osip. *Selected Essays.* Translated by Sidney Monas. Austin: University of Texas Press, 1977.

Marcuse, Herbert. *The Aesthetic Dimension.* Boston: Beacon Press, 1978.

———. *Counterrevolution and Revolt.* Boston: Beacon Press, 1972.

———. *Eros and Civilization.* New York: Vintage Books, 1955.

———. *Five Lectures: Psychoanalysis, Politics and Utopia.* Translated by Jeremy J. Shapiro and S. M. Weber. Boston: Beacon Press, 1970.

———. *Negations.* Boston: Beacon Press, 1968.

———. *One-Dimensional Man: Studies in the Ideology of Advanced Industrial Society.* Boston: Beacon Press, 1964.

———. *Reason and Revolution.* Boston: Beacon Press, 1941.

Marx, Karl. *Early Writings.* Translated by R. Livingstone and G. Benton. New York: Vintage Books, 1975.

———. *The Eighteenth Brumaire of Louis Bonaparte.* New York: International Publishers, 1963.

Melville, Herman. *Moby-Dick.* New York: Hendricks House, 1962.

Merleau-Ponty, Maurice. *Humanism and Terror.* Translated by John O'Neill. Boston: Beacon Press, 1969.

Miller, J. Hillis. *Poets of Reality.* New York: Atheneum, 1969.

Miller, J. Hillis, ed. *William Carlos Williams: A Collection of Critical Essays.* Englewood Cliffs, N.J.: Prentice-Hall, 1966.

Munk, Erica, ed. *Brecht.* New York: Bantam Books, 1972.

Nee, Victor. *The Cultural Revolution at Peking University.* New York: Monthly Review Press, 1969.

Nietzsche, Friedrich. *Basic Writings of Friedrich Nietzsche.* Edited and translated by Walter Kaufmann. New York: Modern Library, 1968.

———. *The Portable Nietzsche.* Edited and translated by Walter Kaufmann. New York: Viking, 1968.

———. *The Will to Power.* Edited by Walter Kaufmann. Translated by Walter Kaufmann and R. J. Hollingdale. New York: Vintage, 1967.

O'Brien, Conor Cruise. "Passion and Cunning." In *TriQuarterly*, no. 23/24 (Winter–Spring 1972).

O'Hara, Frank. *Jackson Pollock.* New York: George Braziller, 1959.

Pascal, Blaise. *Pensées.* Edited by H. S. Thayer. Translated by William F. Trotter. New York: Washington Square Press, 1965.

Payne, Robert. *The Life and Death of Lenin.* New York: Simon & Schuster, 1964.

Plato. *The Republic.* Translated by Francis Cornford. New York: Oxford University Press, 1945.

Pound, Ezra. *The Cantos of Ezra Pound.* New York: New Directions Books, 1972.

Praz, Mario. *The Romantic Agony.* London: Oxford University Press, 1970.

Reich, Charles A. *The Greening of America.* New York: Bantam Books, 1970.

Rilke, Rainer Maria. *Duino Elegies.* Translated by J. B. Leishman and Stephen Spender. New York: Norton, 1939.

Rosenberg, Harold. *The Anxious Object.* New York: New American Library, 1966.

———. *Artworks and Packages.* New York: Dell, 1969.

———. *The Tradition of the New.* New York: McGraw-Hill, 1965.

Sartre, Jean-Paul. *What Is Literature?* Translated by Bernard Frechtman. New York: Harper & Row, 1965.

Séjourne, Laurette. *Burning Water.* Translated by Irene Nicholsen. New York: Vanguard Press, 1956.

Shakespeare, William. *The Tragedy of Hamlet, Prince of Denmark.* Edited by Edward Hubler. New York: New American Library, 1973.

Sobel, Lester A. *Political Terrorism.* New York: Facts on File, 1975.

Solomon, Robert C., ed. *Nietzsche.* Garden City, N.Y.: Doubleday Anchor, 1973.

Sontag, Susan. *Styles of Radical Will.* New York: Farrar, Straus, Giroux, 1969.

Sorel, Georges. *Reflections on Violence.* Translated by T. E. Hulme. New York: Peter Smith, 1941.

Stevens, Wallace. *The Collected Poems.* New York: Alfred A. Knopf, 1964.

———. *The Necessary Angel.* New York: Vintage Books, 1951.

Tolstoy, Leo. *War and Peace.* Translated by Louise Maude and Aylmer Maude. New York: Simon & Schuster, 1942.

Unger, Roberto. *Knowledge and Politics.* New York: Free Press, 1975.

Vico, Giambattista. *The New Science of Giambattista Vico.* Translated by Thomas Bergin and Max Fisch. Ithaca, N.Y.: Cornell University Press, 1970.

Walter, E. V. *Terror and Resistance: A Study of Political Violence.* New York: Oxford University Press, 1969.

Weil, Simone. *Waiting for God.* New York: Harper & Row, 1951.

West, Don. *Sacrifice unto Me.* New York: Pyramid Books, 1974.

Wheelwright, E. L., and McFarlane, B. *The Chinese Road to Socialism.* New York: Monthly Review Press, 1970.

Wilde, Oscar. *The Portable Oscar Wilde.* Edited by Richard Aldington. New York: Viking Press, 1946.

Willett, John, ed. and trans. *Brecht on Theater.* New York: Hill & Wang, 1964.

Williams, William Carlos. *The Collected Earlier Poems.* New York: New Directions Books, 1966.

———. *The Collected Later Poems.* New York: New Directions Books, 1963.

———. *Paterson.* New York: New Directions Books, 1963.

———. *Pictures from Brueghel and Other Poems.* New York: New Directions Books, 1962.

Yeats, William Butler. *The Collected Poems.* New York: Macmillan, 1956.